All Things Ella

ELLA ANNE KOCIUBA

This book is dedicated to my mother and father.

I hope what you read here doesn't frighten you too much. It even startles me sometimes, but you both have given me the courage, the strength and the wisdom to live my life to the fullest, to always be myself, and for that I thank you from the deepest parts of my heart; I truly do mean that.

It is also dedicated to my best friend and other half. She has always been there to share giggles with, is always up for a gym session, and has always been there to have intellectual talks with in this beautifully tainted world.

She has helped me to find some peace with my demons, and has supported me in fighting the good fight.

Sara Glenn, thank you for all that you are and all that you do.

I feel like it would be wrong of me if I didn't mention the help from Ed Collins, who not only offered his guidance to me but helped assist me in gathering up my efforts, edit my work, and turned my dream of publishing a book into a reality. Thank you man.

And, of course, it is dedicated to my beloved friends and fans.

Thank you for the support.

CONTENTS

ACKNOWLEDGMENTS

I could write out all of the names of those who have supported me, who have had constant faith in me, and who have loved me even when I was dark and lost. But doing so would take about a year and a half.

No matter how small or how big your part has been in my journey, know that I am forever grateful to you for providing me with your shoulders, whether it was literally or figuratively. I probably wouldn't have made it to this point in my life without so many of you, so this goes out to you.

This also goes out to anyone who struggles with an eating disorder, self-image issues, lives in chronic pain, or to those who strive for greatness.

Finally, all those of you who are up for discovering your inner strength: this is for you.

Cover photo photographer: Richard Riccardi

* Some names have been changed for confidentiality reasons but all accounts and stories are true, you have my word on that.

CHAPTER 1
INTRODUCTION

Well this is an introduction, so just read it.

Deliverance (noun):

The action of being rescued or set free: "prayers for deliverance".

- Oxford American Writer's Dictionary

Don't just skip over my introduction, pretty please. I'm guilty of doing of it with every other book I pick up, I'll admit it, but it would be very wise of you to read this.

It will explain why I have written my story so sporadically, a little bit of why I am the way I am and why I do the things I do. Plus, this section here is where I tell you just who I am in my own words.

My memory has been damaged dramatically for years, and as I searched back through all the scar tissue to share my story with you, I realized just how difficult this was going to be.

And if you're expecting to receive a feel good vibe from this story, think again. This is perhaps the rawest I can get with my emotions, and it might be a Kleenex box read for some. My heart is splattered all over the next few pages.

Judge me, learn from me, but now you'll really know me.

Oh and you might also read this in one sitting, so soak it in.

Bite your lip; swallow.

I would first like to apologize. I'm sorry for the crude language. My parents did not teach me to speak this way, I just don't like to sugarcoat my expressions. I'm rough, I'm blunt, and sometimes I'm rude, but I'm me. I will walk straight through that bush and eat that damn honey. And let me tell ya, it's fucking delicious.

My mother and father *did*, however, teach me to be honest, to always work hard, to be myself, to listen closely, and to never stop respecting others. These simple guidelines are something I would advise anyone to follow. If you do these things, your life will be fantastic, trust me.

Secondly, I simply ask that for the time being you do not pity or even envy me, because just like every cliché story out there I overcame an obstacle that quickly challenged me with the worst, but slowly developed me into my best.

I did not write this book so you could 'poor baby' me or even feel jealous, which, honestly, you really shouldn't. I am on the same ground as you, I drink the same water and have the same needs, just like everyone else; but in a very tragic way, I became special.

I do not consider myself famous, because I have not done anything historically astonishing. History books will not carry my name but if they do, let's bake a cake cause that's neat.

Years from now my adventures will be forgotten. At least I think they will.

However, I hope that the teachings of my story do motivate some amongst you to change your lives for the better, to be brave enough to be yourselves, to have the courage and the strength to test your limits, and to fight the good fight just as the journey I have traveled on has done for me.

Thirdly, I'd like to warn you that my mind likes to wander, so this book shall wander too. This is the first of many books to come, so bear with me, I'm just getting my feet wet.

To give a one sentence summary, this book covers me growing up through my back struggle, my eating disorder issues, and everything personal in between up to the end of 2014.

I wrote this book at the age of 21, and as I told many of my peers, "I'm writing a book, it's my story of how I got to where I am now". Some looked at me and asked "Why not wait until you're older", and others nodded with pride. "This will change the world, Ella".

Well, that's why I wrote this. I wrote this not for someone to give me puppy eyes and hug me, "oh so sorry for your pain Ella". No. I wrote this so that those who are lost can find themselves again.

It may be dark, insightful, vulgar, hard to read at times, upsetting and even confusing, but this is my story.

So many others share this demon that I possess, and suffer from eating disorders. It may actually even be comfortable for you. You may believe you are in control, but you're not; nor will you ever truly get over it.

But this book is here for you, for your family, for the world, and for me. I want to help those who are like me; and those who are not.

While I may not have been the sickest of the sick, or had my haunting troubles for long, I still live it daily, and have a story to share.

My story is one of which I believe can save someone. I want to save you and I want to save myself.

Give me mud. Give me scars.

I've never really been too good at talking about myself, but I feel like that's a common thing that common people say and I don't consider myself to be all that common; in fact, exactly the opposite.

Throughout middle school and high school I was never number one on the team. I was never the one making headlines in the newspapers and strangers did not even know my name, especially my last name, no one could pronounce it anyways.

And so we get that shit cleared, it's pronounced ko-SEE-bah.

Just like a dim candlelight, I flickered quietly in the background of my peers.

Later on in life I found out that it is adversity that not only destroys me but also gives me an undeniable strength to help me better my life.

So, this is how I did it, this is how I overcame the impossible and all I was given was the chance to do it, whether I believed in myself or not.

What you are about to read is all true.

It is a story about how I, Ella Anne Kociuba, beat the odds and made a name for myself when all I did was fail, fail, and fail again. Guess what, I am successful because of my failures. I am going to give away my "secret" to success, but really I'm just going to vent to you about how hard life can be and tell you how I coped with it.

Oh how dramatic that sounds! Trust me though, I have valuable teachings to give here. And yeah, I know that I am "only twenty-one". Get over it.

Even though I am young and my story is still being written, I figured that I would start this bullshit already and help someone who is struggling like I once did to pick their feet up and live their lives bravely, even when the shit hits the fan.

I truly believe that my purpose in life is to help other's find their purpose through their struggles, so in the next few chapters you will read all about my life's struggles and victories as well as just exactly what it took for me to turn a negative into a positive. I share it for the simple, honest reason that I want to help better this world, and help better myself.

I was going nowhere good with the route I found myself on, but the way that I see it is that if you want to get stronger you must first be broken down in some sort of fashion. That is how we truly grow.

I've been broken down, or what feels that way, several times and at times it has felt very premature for my age. However, "normality" varies from individual to individual so labeling aspects of my life as "normal" or "not normal" wouldn't technically be fair. Besides, let's face it, life *is* really unfair and if you haven't gotten that reality check yet, trust me, it's coming and you better pay up.

I threw down my money order with this book so to speak and within its pages I give you my testament to building an unbeatable mindset and outlook on life. This outlook is filled with an undeniable potential to be something great, and with a mature acknowledgment that negatives can become positives. It is an outlook enabling you to see obstacles as lessons, and a life full of courage to be yourself even if that really sheds some light on your imperfections.

If my flaws in life can help you to better yourself like it has helped me to better my own self, then I am completely okay with being so vulnerable and letting the world see me for who I really am, because after all I want to see the world around me grow.

I'd like to give you some background on how I grew up, where I hail from, and possibly the development of my mind. Even though I honestly don't know for sure how it became this way, I do have some ideas.

Perhaps it was the chronic back pain that put me in and out of wheel chairs, the sudden depression that I denied for so many years, the silent anorexia and bulimia that I struggled with since the age of eighteen. Or perhaps it was the stress of early childhood that crept up on me later. Better yet, maybe it is the pressure of the past living in my present. But honestly, I am a wreck.

Not even my mistakes, which are enriched in justification, can explain the situations that I have encountered.

Like a young colt chomping down at its bit, snarling and flaring its nostrils, and tasting its own blood at the starting line, I too await my stretch of fame.

But little do I know, with the explosion off the starting line also comes the explosion of a breakdown for the whole crowd to see, and as I fall, I am reminded of the potential inside of me. However my weak, little bones are too immature to withstand its ache, and far too fragile to handle its stress, so I crack underneath it, just like that young triple crown winner who we all wanted to do well. After my sprint of fame, I am put down immediately.

There goes my greatness. Life is painfully unfair, you know.

It's not all positive shit that made me positive, it's a lot of the negatives too.

My family and stuff like that is a good place to start, I guess.

I grew up into a family of athletes and, forgive me for bragging for a minute or two but, my brothers are outstanding athletes and their talents varied into several sports throughout their lives. My sister also excelled as a runner in high school. With her tiny figure and delicate face, she was the girl next door. So it was safe to say I had huge shoes to fill.

However, I did not necessarily acknowledge my expectations until my ability to walk became threatened, but we'll get to that point of my life later.

I grew up in a beautiful, loving family, my father didn't abuse me, my mother wasn't mean to me and they are a happily married couple who eat dinner together every night.

My mother is one of the hardest working PE Coaches for fifth and sixth graders I know of, and works at the school that I grew up in. My father is an insanely talented custom home builder who builds and remodels homes all over Austin, Texas. They loved me unconditionally and took care of my siblings and I as best as they could; providing us with good meals, shelter, guidance, and financial support when we needed it.

My father would drive just about every weekend up to Illinois to see my second oldest brother play college football. My mother competed alongside me in many horse races. Their hearts had no limits and they truly did their best to be there for each one of us.

Every holiday was spent with all of us together laughing about old childhood stories, drinking beer and wine while watching the football game and playing card games, then eating huge amounts of food that my wonderful mother spent hours on making.

I come from a family of big eaters, we eat, we drink, we're loud, and we're go getters. I grew up watching my father and brothers get seconds, thirds, and then eat dessert, and my mother frowning down at the brownies she just made, "oh I really shouldn't" but she did anyways. My family eats.

I was always encouraged to eat, to be happy, and to enjoy a drink or two. So I never really cared or thought too much about what or how I ate until I hit eighteen years old.

Often our home lives can cause us to develop depression and expose us to mental disorders, but in my case, it wasn't my family that caused me to become so depressed and to develop an eating disorder. I was never questioned about my weight nor was I told that I must look a certain way by my mother or my father.

Nothing was pressured into me by anything other than my own obsessive desires to be great.

I am the baby of four and my sister, Callie, who is three years older than me was the one that I didn't seem to click with the most due to our differences.

She was an incredibly fast runner in high school and one of our school's top athletes. After graduating she went up to Lubbock, Texas to get her degree as a teacher at Texas Tech University. While attending that University, my sister joined a sorority and did all those cliché party things.

Now if you meet my sister and I, you will never guess that we are related. We are complete opposites and sometimes I love it and sometimes I hate it.

Callie has a tender heart, one to get tripped up easily in chaos, and reacts off of emotions and the simple desire to fit in with others.

Growing up we didn't spend much time together but I always saw her as the beautiful person that she is. One of the biggest things that I admire about my sister is her undeniable ability to be patient with little children and the elderly, something I never seemed to get a good grip of.

My oldest brother, Tyler, is a gentleman that every mother and father on this planet would die to have, and I can honestly say that with no hesitation. Better yet, all of my siblings fall under this category.

Tyler is the only one out of all four of us who got my father's dark Native American skin and black hair. In high school, I believe Tyler or T.K. as we call him was quite the ladies' man. His attractive looks and athleticism brought him great success, and he always worked so incredibly hard.

T.K. has a soft expression and a goofy wildness about him. You could always count on him for a good time, but at the same time he always held a respectful demeanor.

He went off to college at Texas A&M in College Station. At first, he started playing rugby for the Aggies but after two years of playing that, he walked on to the football team and quickly made it into the special teams.

My family and I would attend the games to cheer him on, I'll always remember bragging to my friends that I had a badass brother who played for the Aggies and, even if they lost, I thought it was cool as shit.

Upon graduating college, Tyler surprised our family with the news of joining the Navy. This news broke my mother's heart but made mine smile. Now that's my brother, that's my hero. He went off to the Navy and came back top of his class and better yet, he went off to join the SEALs.

My other brother, Casey, is another idol of mine, actually my biggest and although I will hardly admit it to him, I tried so hard to be just like him growing up. I even went as far as shaving in between my eyebrows because I saw him do it once!

I spent countless night's playing Halo or Call Of Duty with him and his friends, running around the woods with paintball guns, and trying to follow him on his hunts; he literally hung the moon for me.

Casey is one that I can relate to without even trying to, and just like T.K., Casey was a big shot in high school and, hell, he sure was the ultimate football player. He was known for making insane runs and racking up the yards with each game.

Casey was living proof to me of how hard work pays off. People knew his name and papers wrote about him. All of the colleges seemed to want him and I was envious of his talents.

But unfortunately, Casey was cursed with injuries that made him miss out on some very important opportunities that ended up haunting him all the way up into college. He attended Illinois State and played football there.

Casey had the potential, in my opinion, to go to the NFL, he was *that* amazing in my eyes, but just like myself, he found that his body became older than he was.

After playing in Illinois for five years, he graduated and came back to Texas to do his grad school at Texas State, majoring in Criminal Justice. He graduated and dropped the news on my parents that he too was going into the military; Marine Officer school at that. My heart dropped in honor, that's my brother, that's my hero.

Both of my brothers are still currently in service for our country and not a day passes by that I am not thankful for them and what they do, not just for my family, but for this country.

I admired my brothers so diligently that I aspired to walk their steps, to possess their strength and their attitude. I wanted to be as honorable as they were to me.

Be worth it.

Like in all families, there is always one black sheep and I think I became that sheep.

Without hesitation I grew into my edgy personality, my quirky flaws, and sprouted outward into my weird characteristics that differed from my siblings. I stapled up my skin with piercings left and right and colored up my precious flesh with my mind and scars.

Yeah, I became the tattooed, pierced, edgy sibling.

I found out the hard way that I grow well in times of great melancholy and easily became the misunderstood one.

But I enjoyed my differences that brought me into so many complicated situations that I created for myself and besides, I appreciate a good challenge, it's fun.

The tragic combination of my bubbly personality and dangerous tolerance for pain seemed to attract all sorts of wonderful opportunities and my go to approach for reaching perfection was self-destruction.

I am a 5'4", dirty blonde, thick built, quirky female who loves unicorns, axes, big cats, anything with the color teal, White Monster energy drinks, feathers, nut butters, rucksacks, boots, weight lifting, guns, baby seals. . .

Heck, I could go on and on about what puts a smile on my dorky face.

The point is, I am one who walks on no path. I am an odd ball, the weird one, someone who is strange by nature and that is one of my greatest talents in life. I am simply just different.

It is not my strength, it is not my looks, nor is it my sick ability to numb out pain, it is the simple fact that I am standing between failing and failure, I am essentially a grain of sand in your shoe.

I'm not supposed to be here. To the world I am tiny. But to some, I am a huge motivator to check your feet, change your socks, and be thankful for your shoes.

I am a grain of sand in your shoe, feel me alter your souls as you walk through your life.

At the young age of six, I began to compete my Arabian horses in Endurance Riding.

Endurance is an equestrian sport, that is usually held at private ranches or national parks, where horse and rider must complete the marked course as fast as possible all while passing mandatory vet checks. Distances for these events range from twenty-five to one hundred miles long, but I mainly competed in the twenty-five and fifty mile distances.

Riding horses has always come very natural to me and it will always sort of be that way. I can go months without riding, but when I return, everything feels right and comfortable.

Horseback riding was my first love in life and it also provided my first lesson in life: To be grateful for your health and how to look after others.

Once I reached middle school, I began to suffer through some physical restrictions which pushed me into a depression that I denied until after graduating high school where it seemed like I was owning life.

It wasn't long until my dirty habits took a hold of me and I discovered first hand through the constant vomiting, the out of control eating, the crippling back pain, and the hesitation with loving myself and others that I was clinically depressed and that I had issues.

Someone help me.

Hard work was not necessarily hammered into my siblings and me. Needless to say we were just born to work that way. Like freaky robots, we function for a purpose, and work hard until that purpose is achieved. It is the strength of our genetics that have made up such a dangerous will and desire to succeed.

With that being said, my eating disorder was able to tackle me down to the ground due to my genetic makeup of becoming a perfectionist, an extremist, I wanted to be number one regardless of the situation, and I was the hardest critic of my own self.

I do not believe in luck, instead, I believe that in life we encounter situations, and with every situation we encounter there will always be two outcomes, one that will affect you positively and one that will affect you negatively. And sometimes, shit just happens for no reason. No, the good Lord did not break your arm because he loves you. No, the good Lord did not make your wife leave you so that something better can come along. No. It just happened that way.

Constantly there is shit happening in life that we cannot control, and there are things that occur to us that we do not deserve. Yeah, we've all got shit we deal with, whether we want to acknowledge it or not and I'm willing to share mine with you, but by all means, believe whatever you want to believe.

Shit just happens in my opinion.

And I got a lot of shit at a young age.

Inside my mind creeps these demons, you see. They lurk around in the shadows, in the cracks of my skull and inside the imperfections of my mind. They sprout their little rotten roots which splatter their poison all over my grey matter. I'm tainted now with chemicals I cannot comprehend. These demons lay awake and await their attack at any little mistake that I just might happen to make.

I have no control. I find myself scrambling through the mess. Digging deeper. And deeper. Where do I go? I'm after a dark place. One in which no one can find me; a place where I cannot even find my own self. I want to be lost.

I want to be alive. I want so badly to achieve these dreams that haunt me day in and day out. I ache. I strive for it. It is what makes me who I am. Developing me into an outstanding sculpture, one that cannot withstand its own desire.

It pushes me to a new beginning, a new meaning.

Hands tremble.
Fingers blister.
Veins bulge.
Heart races.
Eyes twitch.
Lungs ache.
Legs burn.
Feet numb.
Knees shake.
Back pulses.
Glutes stiffen.

I feel it all. I feel the work. I feel the labor of my desire. I don't just want it, I need it.

A perfectionist at heart, an extremist by nature. That's me. That is my genetic makeup that delivers me to bulimia on a golden platter. Whether I see it or not, my strive for "greatness" is also the same route as self-abuse.

No, no. These voices in my head, go far away, as far away as my goals are to me. I want to touch them and I want to be there with their glory and all, vicious yet honorable I am fearful that I cannot grasp them and I feel like a hopeless dreamer amongst the soreness of my attempts.

I feel lost.

A sideline here. A sideline there. And forgotten I go.
Why is the world so cold?

Do you think I'm crazy yet?
But more importantly do I have your attention yet?

Feel me out here, there's something gorgeous about a breakdown and I want to expose mine to show you that success can be found here, that a struggle is nothing to fear.

I want you to see what I see and feel what I feel, if only for a moment, so that you can get that chance to change your overall path as a human being.

And I really do want to help save others. If I could save someone from experiencing what I have felt, I could go to bed happier.

Let's be grateful.

Let's get weird.

An athlete's worst nightmare is a doctor. Specifically a doctor with a diagnosis of your injury. I face my nightmare often, look it right in the face as it stares back at me.

"What do you want from me?"

All polite and considerate with its deliverance. Those white scrubs and quiet, sole supporting shoes.

"Just fix me already."

Folders cradled in their intelligent arms as they approach your weak little self in the chair. You tremble inside awaiting your news, your heart begins to beat a little bit faster than normal.

"Tell me, tell me, tell me!!"

The control that they possess over your emotions is outrageous at this moment. They hold all of your happiness in their hands, and to them it's no big deal. *But this is my everything.*

Shit man, this is life.

I believe we are all meant for greatness, just some of us have the courage to go after it and to fight for it. And because of that, some of us will become great while so many of us will observe from our very own sidelines, whispering to ourselves "I wish I could do something that great with my life."

Fight the good fight.

"I've got some issues that nobody can see

And all of these emotions are pouring out of me

I bring them to the light for you

It's only right

This is the soundtrack to my life."

-Kid Cudi

CHAPTER 2
BREAKDOWN

The incident that changed my life. And a few others.

My mind is scattered into pieces.

Just like the bones in my body.

Broken and twisted,

My sins have made me wicked.

Although my memory sucks and I cannot remember the exact details of that night, I can recall the majority of it quite well. But just so you know, some fluffy words have been added to help paint the images of my story for your reading pleasure.

So here it is, my account of my downfall.

I am the Triple Crown winner, I am the one who sprints to his let down and falls face first.

Please put the horse down, rider has gone M. I. A.

Enjoy my destruction.

The smell of Socks' sweat soaked deep into the Old English leather as her nostrils vibrated in the bone chilling winter air. She chewed her bit anxiously, pawing at the ground like an enraged bull ready to charge. Her energy floated rapidly into the darkness of the night as we traveled through the woods in such an easy rhythm that it could put an infant to sleep.

It's moments like these where nothing else seems to matter to me. The separation from all the worries of everyday life fades out in such a graceful way that even the deepest of heart aches can be soothed.

At first glance, Socks isn't the prettiest horse you will see out in the pasture. Her coat is woolly all year around. Her face is angular in a masculine way, and she does not carry herself in a high fashion manner like most mares.

Socks was a half saddle bred and half Arab mix which made her trot full of bounce and her spirits obnoxiously high. Luckily she didn't seem to pick up the spooky tendencies Arabian horses generally have, however she did carry their high drive to run.

Socks was a true character and her attitude was one to make a saint become a sailor without hesitation, she did not have an ounce of mercy when it came to low hanging tree branches; and I mean none whatsoever.

When my Mother first bought Socks, her skin clung to her ribs, her hair was matted into thick knots yet she still felt like silk. Even with all the damages from being starved, beaten and neglected, Socks' spirit shined brightly. However, due to Socks' beatings, she didn't allow anyone to touch her forehead. She would immediately shy away at anything that ever came close to her beautiful face.

This horse was special, she came into our lives to better it, and although mine was almost ruined because of our accident together, she taught me many, many things about life. And if I ever see her again, I'll tell her thank you and actually mean it. I will actually feel my heart tear up when I see her gnarled face, for she gave me the greatest thing anyone could ask for: A chance to rise up even after falling so hard. She gave me the mindset to fight.

That night as we rode, I noticed that the land was becoming a bit dull, the trees somehow ceased in their beauty due to my constant glare, and the curvature of the dirt path did not come as a pleasant surprise anymore.

But the motion of Socks and I riding as one, now that could never become dull to me. Never once will it fade in excitement, nor will it ever disappoint my senses.

In a way, my time with the horses was the only time I felt like I was my true self, due to the lack of pressures, expectations, and eyes upon me. In those moments with them, I am simply free to just be.

We headed home and, as we came to the final hill, I urged her into a gallop. Socks responded and opened up her gait as we flew forward together as one. My body clutched close to hers as we accelerated, closing my eyes as the wind blew into my face.

It was that kind of moment, the one where you feel invincible, as if nothing else matters in the world but this very moment I'm in. Although it is about to destroy me and everything I enjoy, this moment is my ultimate getaway and it is also one of the greatest moments I will ever endure.

It was the moment my life changed forever.

Give me mud. Give me scars.

I have found that one of the hardest things to accept in life is disappointment.

It is a slow, toxic burn, one that will tear your heart into pathetic strips, like a mute paper shredder; just going through the motions that it is programmed to do. No one wants to accept the emotion nor does one want to claim it as theirs. So we simply push the 'ON' button and go about our business, as if the heaviness of our failures does not weaken our souls.

At times later on in my life I found myself fighting the aggressive feeling of disappointment about the way things are. It is the hardest pill for me to swallow until it occurs to me that this pill is just a placebo and I have no reason to actually feel disappointed anymore. I realize that I don't need to take this toxic medicine. This isn't how it has to be. There is greatness to come of this, I have always been great, and I need to start believing in myself.

Bite your lip. Swallow.

A deer jumped out in front of Socks while she was in mid stride. She halted immediately and dropped back onto her hocks. My petite body flew forward onto her neck. I lost the stirrups, I lost the reins, and I lost my body.

In the next milliseconds, my life changed. She reared up, my body flew backwards onto the rocks below, and I was left to lie motionless.

Darkness.

My heart was pounding inside my skull so violently I felt as if I was a sick animal being drug tested. My eyes were stitched back with thorns and burned as if acid had been dumped into them. Screeching in pain.

Perhaps it was demons inside me coming out, but unfortunately it wasn't, it was my life getting fucked up and in an instant my entire body was depleted of its strength.

I do not know how long I was out for but it must not have been for too long. When I came to, Socks stood before me while I tried to grip onto reality.

Where? What? How? Why?

Small pebbles and clumps of dried dirt were embedded into my soft skin. My mind was covered in a heavy fog and the pain in my spine was something so incredibly new to me that I didn't even know what to make of it. It was just so amazingly painful that my heart raced at speeds that I couldn't seem to handle and suddenly it occurred to me. . .

I had fallen. Not just at this very moment but for years to come.

I was twelve years young at the time of my accident.

It started with chiropractors. A simple readjustment for my back pain should be the fix. Or so we think. I go to a chiropractor for a while and we see no progress, just an aggressive decrease in my mobile skills and an increase in pain. So we decide to try other approaches.

I am sent to Physical Therapists and to other back specialists where I am put into metal braces that go from my collar bone to my pelvic bone. I am dosed with heavy medications, and attempts with physical therapy to ease the situation but everything fails to do so.

I get x-rays, MRI's, CT scans and everything comes up okay. So I'm told.

"You're just sore Ella, you'll be okay".

But I wasn't okay.

I was becoming increasingly crippled by the day, and after a couple months of gradual decrease in my overall life, my parents found themselves scrambling for some serious help.

It had been about four months since the accident and I was getting more and more consistent with not walking, not sleeping, not eating, not smiling, and not being what a twelve year old kid should be like.

I am misunderstood.

I am depressed.

I am hurting.

The woman's face was weathered with wrinkles and caked with makeup. However, she seemed to possess a calming look about her as she talked to my parents.

I sat in the chair up against the wall with my arms holding my body tightly, sniffling ever so gently in attempts to keep my tears unseen. But my eye juice seemed to be a constant flow, for my pain was out of control these days. Nonetheless, I watched and I listened patiently to her as she spilled out information in regards to bettering my health, to curing me. She had my full attention collected in her stressful face and dramatic hand gestures because I wanted to be healthy more than anything.

Her blonde hair had an excellent bounce to it as it swooped in and around her face, the heavy mascara flickered off of her smothered eyelashes, and her coffee stained teeth hid behind her cherry blossom pink lips.

"We'll start decompression next session, for the x-ray shows that your daughter has two slipping discs and three discs that are herniated."

The woman talked with her hands too much at this point and my eyes couldn't seem to keep up. I was instantly overloaded with substance, and before I knew it, we were leaving the doctor's office with a game plan.

Decompression was going to fix me, I was told. "Things will get better, don't you worry."

I returned back to her office for the next couple of weeks where she performed decompression on me and then laser therapy.

Decompression is a method where the patient lies down on the table and two straps are put onto the body. One strap is secured tightly around the hips while the other strap is around the ribcage, the machine then slowly pulls apart, giving traction from both directions.

I was still twelve years young, and still crying for my mother to help me out of the bathtub from time to time. I was still taking narcotics just to make it through the day and all of this became the regular for me. It was all becoming numb and for some odd reason, I accepted it. I acknowledged that that was the life for me and it was painful.

My life is pain.
My head is confusion.
My body is ruined.
It is what it is. Right?

Christmas time was approaching and the usual joyfulness is present all around me, but not within me.

I was a dark creature, lurking behind my classmates, missing out on memories to remember and friendships to make. I was losing sleep and most importantly I was losing my mind.

Twice a week I was getting decompression treatment done, I was getting my spine pulled slowly apart by a machine and I was told repeatedly not to worry, that I would be okay.

My mother would pull me out of school early to beat traffic and get me to the clinic. My treatments lasted about thirty minutes, and afterwards I laid down on another table, as lasers beamed into my spine in an attempt to ease the muscle spasms.

Every time I laid down during the decompression treatments, while my body slowly got pulled apart, my mind would go blank and I would glare at the TV as Everybody Loves Raymond played on the screen. My mother sat nearby skimming Prevention or some sort of cooking magazine. That was my life and I really didn't get it.

On one particular day that I was at the clinic, my chiropractor left to go Christmas shopping. Only the young aide remained to go forth with my treatment.

On that day they told me that they were increasing the resistance pull by fifty pounds.

I laid down on the table and the aide strapped me in tightly. The session began and so did Everybody Loves Raymond. Little did I know what was about to occur to me. I laid there awake, awaiting yet another moment that would change my life completely in a matter of seconds, and as the machine began to pull me with more force from both sides I began to feel it.

I felt uncertainty consume the flow of my body and I felt everything in my back getting ripped apart.

Enjoy my reconstruction.

Imagine what a guitar string appears to look like when it is stretched too much. Its fine fibers begin to sporadically split apart in different ways one by one. At the same time, imagine a devious creature getting a fine needle to strum the splitting fibers. Well, that was the tendons and muscles in my back. That was what it felt like as I was being ripped apart by that machine.

The screams and cries escaping my throat sounded like they were from hell and they echoed louder than any of the other dangerous voices that filled my fucked up skull.

My entire body felt a sudden vibration throughout it and then nothing. I went completely numb and a hot sweat flooded over my body instantly but my face stayed ice cold white.

I passed out and dipped into the darkness. My body flopped down and I appeared to have no life in me.

The last thing that I remember seeing before the lights went out is my mother screaming for the nurse, scrambling for help and scanning the machine for the power button. The nurse came rushing in with no certain knowledge as to how to stop it and only brought more panic with which to fill the room.

I was a moment's notice away from the machine pulling me far past the point of being repaired. Within a matter of seconds I was looking at being paralyzed for life.

Suddenly, the machine stopped and so did my body, it stopped functioning properly.

Boy is life painfully annoying now.

My bed began to swallow me and it became my only surface area of life. But even there, there was no true life. I attempted to get lost underneath the sheets as if my escape could be that easy. I drifted in and out of heavy sleeping due to more heavy medications I was now taking religiously. I was completely bed ridden for the next week with little to no feeling in my legs and neck.

Two days after the incident, the chiropractor confessed to us that she had never seen the final images from my MRI's and was actually not even certified to look at them. Her explanations for why she increased the weight on the traction so much and for why she left that day were totally unjustified.

Instead of suing her, my father walked in and demanded a full refund of our money and for her to quit her practice, all while his baby girl seemed to be rotting away in bed.

My life, oh my life how it felt so ruined at the time.

Give me mud. Give me scars.

The noise of static was now the description of my life. It was filled with a severe loss of connection, painfully annoying images that glitched before my eyes, and it appeared to have no purpose whatsoever anymore.

What eats me the most about that time of my life is the acceptance I had of it. The fact that I let the blankets of negativity wrap around me and even with their heaviness, I was still so cold.

Get me away from here, far, far away.

Just like my goals, far away from me, that's where I want to be.

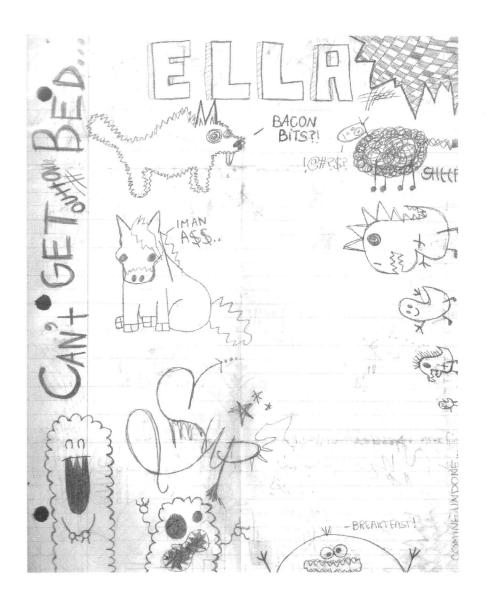

I can remember standing there softly crying in that asshole of a doctor's office as they fitted the hard plastic brace onto my torso. Pulling the straps ever so tightly around me. Slightly jerking my body to the left and to the right, the fucking pain was so real that I can't even tell the doctor to stop or to go easier on it.

The next doctor found in my x-rays that I had fractures of the L4 and the L5 vertebrae, one appearing to be older than the other.

So he cast a brace to fit my back in order to help my spine to realign and to mend on its own.

My mother watched from the corner of the room, her hands over her lips. Trying not to cry or show any sadness, she made attempts at jokes to lighten the mood.

My head just hung low. I couldn't even pick it up to look at the doctor in the face and ask him if I was going to be okay or if I really had to wear this.

I didn't even understand where I was at in life and quite frankly it was a disgusting feeling that I couldn't seem to explain to those around me.

I feel sad. I feel lonely. I feel ugly. I feel pain all the time.

I was instructed to wear the brace twenty-two hours out of the day with only two hours off for the next two months. The brace went up from my pelvic bone to my collar bone and allowed no flexibility to my body.

As if I wasn't sad enough already, I was now trapped inside a hard plastic brace that really demonstrated to everyone, including me, just how weak I truly was.

I tried to hide the brace by wearing hoodies during school and ignored its restrictions. Sure enough it became even harder than ever to stay there in school. The hard plastic seats in class caused me to wind up crying every day.

Every damn day I cried in pain with such great confusion.

"Why, oh why am I here?"

Eventually the brace damaged the nerves that go into my neck and right arm which caused me to have constant muscle cramps and pinched nerves that randomly went off, incapacitating me.

A few times in particular, that I recall, it paralyzed me right there in the classroom in front of my classmates, and I was left there sobbing as my teachers rushed to pick me up. They carried me to the nurse, as my friends watched me fall apart.

Two weeks of wearing the brace went by and we threw in the towel. It had just made me little by little more disabled.

The doctor at the time looked over at my mother and told her "she's just being a big baby." As soon as his words left his mouth, I questioned my own self-worth. Life was so damned painful and perhaps it was true, I couldn't handle its demands.

My mother exchanged some colorful words with the doctor and we quit going to him, only to move onward aimlessly in the hopes of finding someone else who was full of good and had the right help that we needed.

My parents were about to rip the hair out of their heads as they looked down at me lying on the couch with my face swollen from tears and my body limp as a wet noodle.

"What do we do now?"

My mother got in contact with the Children's Hospital of Austin and found a back specialist by the name of John Williams who was one of the best spinal surgeons in Texas. I went to him days later and our first visit there in his office ended up being five hours long. He sat there and listened to the list of doctors I had gone to, the medications I had consumed, the practices performed on me and most importantly, he listened to the that pain I had.

"There's something else going on here, something real serious. I believe we need to go in for exploratory surgery, or your daughter will eventually be crippled."

I remember seeing those words flow from his lips, they were graceful but they were also just so damn terrifying.

Crippled.
Surgery.
Exploratory.

I hated hearing them but at the same time I loved it. I loved the fact that I was perhaps going to break a barrier and grow from it. I wanted a breakdown and I wanted it now. Give it to me. I began to tremble.

Leading up to this point in time life led me to believe that I was already done and all I ever ached for was to become numb.

We finally found the right doctor to help me and it had only taken five physicians of various practices to suffer through.

Surgery was planned two weeks out from the initial first visit and time passed more quickly than ever to that moment before operation day. I can hardly even remember what life was like in the days leading up to my procedure, but what I do remember is feeling both terrified and ready at the same time.

I was awake for the majority of the night. I could feel my veins shaking in a struggle to keep up with my heart as it pumped at insane speeds while the arteries in my body sporadically tried to dispose my plasma to my system.

"Is this poison or is this my demons shaking me up?"

No, it was neither, this was just pure fear flowing throughout my body and I let it spoon feed my pathetic ass pounds of its depressing emotions. All I could envision was the possibility of this surgery ending with me being paralyzed.

The clock ate the minutes up like a fat puppy under the dinner table, licking up delicious crumbs from the ground. There is no time to waste, and then just like that it was time for the hospital.

My mother came up to my bed and sat down next to me, her soft hands touched my cheeks as she leant in to kiss my forehead. "It's time to go

Ella. You got everything you need?" I laid there for a few minutes. Finally, after accepting my fate, I reached out my hands to her and she assisted me up.

The car ride to the hospital that morning was black and silent. The reality of my future was sinking in.

"Why, oh why am I here?"

My father pulled up to the front doors. They glowed in a safe way, their intentions to warm your soon-to-be cold bones. "Here are the doors to better things, come on in you weak humans."

I could feel the fear pushing up against my skin, its pulse sickening me as my mother helped me into a wheelchair.

"Why, oh why am I here?"

Rolling through the obnoxiously bright lights, the smell of plastic gloves and blood floating through the air filled my nostrils, and the beeps of monitors filled my ears.

I entered my room where the nurses smiled at me. They slightly touched my shoulders, and nodded to my parents. My eyes welled up with tears. I was suddenly at a tragic loss of words and it struck me that this was it.

Destroy me.
Fix me.

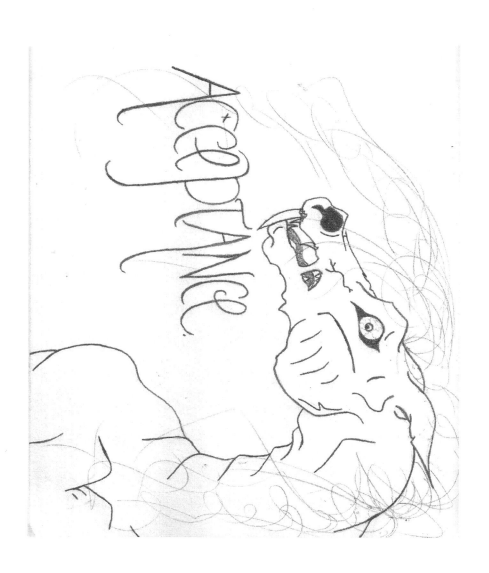

One nurse opened up a book of different gas flavors.

"What flavor would you like? We got bubble gum, cotton candy, strawberry, watermelon..."

I stared at the book full of colored tabs and labels for all these different kinds of fruity shit.

"Why you gotta offer me such fruity shit lady? Can I not fall asleep to the smell of bacon?"

I was in tears already and I couldn't seem to stop my body from trembling as my little fingers pointed towards the tab of the obnoxiously fake painting of a watermelon. She smiled.

"Oh! Good choice, that one's my favorite."

The transfer from my wheelchair to table took five different nurses. As they picked me up to lay me down onto the table I looked over at my mother and father standing there trying to smile to keep things light. I didn't want to leave them. I didn't want to go but at the same time I wanted to go. I wanted to be free of my pain.

My mother leaned down to kiss my forehead again. Man, there's just something so intimate and safe about forehead kisses that I will forever adore. Her dry lips left my forehead and our fingers let go of each other. I looked back up at her, my eyes full of tears.

"I love you."

"I love you too, we'll be right here when you wake up."

My father smiled and told me that he was proud of me and at the time I didn't really get why, but now I understand the reasoning behind his smile and words that day. He saw me not as the broken angel that I felt like, but an angel that had already risen against all odds and even with my broken wings, I could still fly. I could still do great things.

Take me back.
Take me away.

As they rolled me into the operating room, I was filled with fear, and my eyes began to wander around the room. I saw all of the knives and tools which caused my heart to race and nausea to fill up my body.

The gas mask was put over my face. That shitty, fake-ass smell of watermelon absorbed my face and 5, 4, 3......

Darkness.

While undergoing my exploratory surgery, Dr. Williams discovered something incredible about my spine which uncovered the reason behind the chronic pain I was experiencing and of all the failed trials and errors with past doctors.

Now, I've always believed that I was made to be special enough to become something great, and I would be able to change the world with only the story of that greatness that I would possess.

Needless to say, my suspicion of being something special delivered itself on a golden platter and my chance to change the world came forth to me as the discovery of my heartache is revealed.

I was born with a birth defect where my spine was never connected to my sacrum.

The reason why so many people never saw this was due to the simple fact that our bodies are quite astonishing with their coping methods. My body at a young age had tried to repair itself by building a huge block of bone.

However my body's attempts to fix itself had also hidden the separation in the spine and also hidden the full extent of the fractures in the L4 and L5 vertebrae in my spine.

I was also suffering from spondylolisthesis, which is a condition where the vertebrae slips out of the spinal column. I had this going on with four of my vertebrae in the lumbar region of my spine.

So the nine and a half hour procedure left me with four titanium rods and six screws drilled into my spine and sacrum to reconnect me. They also bone-grafted parts of my hip to fix the L4 and L5 break and realigned the vertebrae that were slipping out.

Now I was part bionic and it was time for me to move on with my life.

"Why, oh why am I here?"

Enjoy my revolution.

The familiar sounds of beeping filled my ears but something not so familiar was inside me raging. I heard my name being said repeatedly as I tried to pry my eye lids open.

Everything felt terrible and confusing.

"Where am I?"

Outside my closed world there shined the bright florescent lights glaring down into my soft pupils. Faces that I could not identify hovered above me.

And then suddenly it hit me. It hit me in a harsh second. The pain. The metal in my spine. The incision in my back tissue was saying hello so loudly that I could not help but let the screams leave my mouth. The pain was so unreal that I could not bear it. I began to sob uncontrollably, reaching my arms out for help. I saw my father not far from me.

"Daddy, help me!"

The pain radiated all throughout my pathetic body as the nurses scrambled around me and injected me with more morphine.

Back into the darkness I go.

I awoke later in ICU with my mother and father on one side of the table and a nurse on the other. My parents were holding my hand as the nurse instructed me to sit up.

"Wait, what? Excuse me, you want me to sit up? Is that a joke?"

My back felt disgustingly heavy as all sorts of pain varying from sharp stabs to vibrating aches shot throughout my spine and into the rest of my body. I strain forward crying.

"I can't do it, I can't do it!"

But with assistance from so many others, I finally sat up only to have my breath taken away from me. The pain was making me sick and I couldn't seem to control my crying. But I sat up for them. I sat up for me. Everyone smiled at me and congratulated me.

"Yeah, but I hate you all right now."

I looked around at everyone. "This is terrible" I thought, "I don't want this anymore". I stared at the nurse's hands touching me delicately as she guided me back down slowly onto my back. I passed out in a matter of milliseconds as they put another IV in my arm. I hate needles.

I spent the next ten days relearning how to walk, sleeping in misery, awaking in misery, crying for comfort and being forced to sit up and get used to metal in my spine every couple of hours.

My family and only one of my close friends came to visit me in the hospital bringing flowers, candy and cards. It's times like these where you learn just how true others' hearts are.

The beeping of my monitors filled my ears as the heat of my pain absorbed my face. I laid there and, with each day that passed by, I slowly came to terms with just how long my journey back would take.

Unfortunately, my time spent in the hospital is hard to remember clearly due to the heavy medications and the amount of sleeping that I did, but there are a few profound moments that I can recall vividly.

Like the time I walked for the first time with my walker with its soft tennis balls on its feet, and my IV's and monitor machine on wheels next to me. It was so simple, yet so hard.

"One foot in front of the other, let's go Ella, you got this."

They made me walk every day, the nurses surrounded me and brought me my walker, hooked up my wires so they didn't drag on the ground and followed me with smiling faces as I try to walk.

"Just to the door and back, you can do it."

I didn't have too many complications post-surgery. I did suffer from a minor blood clot that caused me to have high fever for a couple of days, other than that, I took my surgery like a boss.

Coming home wasn't any better for me. Although the environment and feel of home is always an instant comfort, it was not enough to ease me for I was still absorbed by the exotic pain that I felt and crushed by the lack of life inside me.

Every day my mother would take me for walks to the barn, and every day I got closer to making it farther than before. Eventually I could make it to the edge of the fence to feel my horse's nose.

In my opinion, a horse's nose is his or her best feature. It's unbelievably soft and full of such strength, yet at the same time provides so much comfort.

Socks stretched out her neck over the fence and its electric wires. She sniffed my hands and picked up her ears towards me. I'm sure she'd been wondering where I'd been and I began to feel guilty.

"I miss you girl."

Affectionate nuzzling could only ease so few of my aches, I was still left feeling so alone in my pain.

"Why, oh why am I here?"

"You might not be able to ride your horse again."

"You might not be able to play sports again."

"You cannot afford a bad fall."

As expected, my journey to becoming "normal" again was one that took what felt like forever, and despite my patience I couldn't seem to get over the fact that I could not do what I used to do.

I went back to a static life and found myself just going through the motions in physical therapy twice a week for the next year and a half. They get me to do mobility work, extensive stretches, scar tissue manipulation and pain management.

The process of weaning me off the heavy pain medications challenged me more mentally than it did physically.

My hunger for greatness started with my physical therapist simply telling me to walk until my pain got to a level five on a scale of one to ten and then to walk back home. I was determined to regain my strength and life back so I began to walk every day, and with each passing day, I made it a few steps farther.

Each little walk took everything out of me and I found myself shaking at the end of them. Even a 100 meter walk was a nightmare for me to travel, but it was a goal I saw as already mastered.

I got this.

After a couple of weeks of walking farther and farther, I was finally able to walk a mile by myself and it was a huge turning point for me spiritually.

A mile at a time
I walk by myself.
A mile at a time
I walk until I found myself.
And all it took was a mile alone.

There was more for me out there in life and I needed to go get it, I needed to go become it and despite its distance from me I went after it.

Despite my doctor's words declaring that sports weren't in my future, I began to sculpt a performing masterpiece from the scraps of so many hopeless efforts. It fueled me like no other force could because I wasn't about to have someone tell me what I could and couldn't do with my very own life.

So with their words of limitations floating amongst the aches in my spine, I decided to prove the predictions of my life to be false.

Needless to say, the drive that I developed from my surgery was something so profound and organic to my character that it seemed to terrify those around me. But secretly I enjoyed the fear I brought, for I was on a mission. My mission was simple:

"Don't waste my second chance to become something great in life."

BE GREAT.

The following is written by my mother and it is what she saw through her own eyes. Her account of my process through my back injury, the doctors, and the procedure itself.

Life has a way of placing unexpected and sometimes deeply unwelcome challenges squarely in our path. What follows is my experience with Ella's unwelcome challenge that arrived squarely in the path of her 7th grade year.

My husband and I were truly gifted with four beautiful children who were all exceptionally talented with athletic abilities.

Our youngest, Ella, grew up as a night owl, with a wonderful sense of humor and terrific strength.

Ever since she was about 5 years old, she would move all of her heavy cargo furniture around in her room, for a new look, on a regular basis. She did this so often that the neighbor's girl told us she didn't want to come play anymore because all Ella wanted to do was move furniture!

Ella shared my love of horses and started riding with me when she was only two. She had a bad accident at the age of 4, when our big 16 hand gelding, Chuffy, ran off with her in saddle. She fell and ended up with a terrible concussion. On arrival home from the hospital, she wanted to go to the barn to tell Chuffy she loved him anyway.

It was this love of horses that helped identify a serious problem that always seemed to be in disguise.

When Ella began athletics in Junior High, she complained that her back was hurting during volleyball and cross country season. Trying not to be the over-reactive parents, we told her it was probably only sore muscles and she needed to stretch more.

As her activity progressed to basketball, she had a sharp pain in her back that resulted in concern for her health. We took her to the hospital where they took x-rays. All came back fine. No problems with her spine.

Backed with this information we assured her it was only sore muscles and she needed to work harder at warming up before exerting herself in sports.

Next came track and field. Starting blocks were miserable. Ella's speed and stamina were not the same. The only constant was the love of the horse and her riding.

Maybe, I thought, she just wasn't meant to be an athlete like the others. She was gifted as an artist and I tried to compliment her on those skills. However, I clearly remember one June evening under the stars while camping with our endurance horses. She was crying that there really was something wrong with her back. That her back was always hurting. Relying on the information from the doctor I tried to tell myself she was going to be just fine.

However, I soon enlisted the help of a chiropractor to reduce her back pain. I noticed Ella didn't ride as much as usual. This was another hint of trouble that I tried to suppress.

The next fall came in her 8th grade year. She was running cross country and we noticed her running form was horrible, and was leaning forward in an unusual way. I started to feel like there was something that we didn't know about her back. She was one of the last in the pack to finish her races, but she would never give up.

Also quite notable, was her lack of time in the saddle. It hurt to ride the horse. I knew this was not normal. Maybe she couldn't be a starter in volleyball, but she always wanted to ride her horse. If she wasn't riding as much, I knew there must be something wrong. I wanted to believe she was just fine, that it was just an excuse for not being successful as she wanted to be in athletics. However, there was that nagging feeling deep inside that would raise its ugly head to warn me that Ella wasn't fine.

About this time, Ella had a terrible fall from her horse, Socks, that sent the pain in her back off the charts. The chiropractor took x-rays and sent us to another doctor in the same profession but who offered something referred to as decompression.

It was this terrible experience from an incompetent doctor that sent Ella spiraling into darkness with pain. We were right there with her. She was rubber-legged and vomiting in pain after about the 4th decompression treatment.

What kind of doctor would leave a young patient hooked up to a machine, with only a high school secretary in charge while she was Christmas shopping on a Friday evening and then never return our phone calls filled with anxiety over Ella's unusual pain?

Panicked and scared, my husband and I rushed her to a back specialist first thing that Monday morning. After her CTI, MRI and further X-rays we learned that she had two fractures both in the L4 and L5 vertebrae and a condition from birth called spondylothesis. One old fracture and one new. Why? I couldn't believe my ears. Why did the old fracture not show up the year before when we were at the hospital with X-rays taken?

The back specialist suggested casting Ella's back to heal correctly. So we got her measured for a specially fitted back cast. I just knew this would fix her. Problem solved. I could look forward with optimism now.

No sports. No horses. Just time for her art skills now. Her pain was unbearable so she was prescribed pain pills. With each visit, there was not any improvement and the narcotics to control the pain kept getting stronger with each different prescription.

That optimism I had felt with the cast was now turning to high anxiety again.

Ella was also prescribed physical therapy. Her right arm began to go numb and she had unusual pains shooting up her spine. Out of frustration the doctor sharply told her that she had a fractured back and it was going to hurt! She needed to "suck it up"... My heart fell and my anger rose. She was vomiting. Was it the narcotics or the pain? Was it the physical therapy? The therapist refused to work on her again after one session of her vomiting everywhere due to the pain.

We had seen four different doctors by this point and no improvement. Ella was continuing to experience more pain. She was missing a lot of school at this point in time. Her father and I were both mentally and spiritually drained.

Early one Monday morning, after a terrible weekend of Ella being so uncomfortable, I called Dell's Children's Hospital and asked for a pediatric back specialist. Everyone was booked for a month out. As I pleaded with the operator that my daughter was in terrible pain and explaining how long this had been going on she found a cancellation and a Dr. John Williams could see her - in an hour!

For the first time, I felt real hope that we could fix Ella! He spent five hours with Ella that day. The first thing he did was throw away all the narcotics and prescribed a much less addictive medicine to control her pain.

He was the first doctor to really listen to Ella and decided that the only way to fix her pain was surgery. His concern about her butt pain led him to believe that there was something else wrong besides the spondylothesis and would do some exploration during surgery to see what might be causing all the pain in the buttocks.

He was in total amazement at all the things Ella had been doing in sports over the past two years considering her condition. He knew she was a strong girl.

With her surgery date set, we began the preparations. Drawing blood for surgery in case she needed it. Relocating her bedroom downstairs. Calling grandparents in Illinois to come help. Calling her school to let them know she would be gone for two months. Taking off 2 months of work to be with her! Praying even harder every night before bed.

The prospect of surgery always scares me, but it also gave me hope that this doctor would be the one to finally rid Ella of her problems. He exuded such confidence in her treatment that it was hard not to be optimistic.

The surgery day arrived. My husband and I waited patiently for the news that Ella was recovering. After 5 hours, the nurse called for us and I was blown away when she said there was a bit of a problem with Ella's back and they had to order two more titanium rods to fix her back. So on went the waiting and the praying for several more hours.

I think that was the longest day of my life. I prayed to God that all we wanted was for our child to be healthy. I would do anything for that to happen.

At end of day they called for one of us to be with Ella in the recovery room. The sight and sound of her overwhelmed me and I couldn't bear it, so my husband had to replace me to be by her side for that first hour. I couldn't stand to see my child in such pain.

We both slept with her in ICU that night, laying on the floor and taking turns sleeping. I found myself drawing on my husband's strength, gentleness and courage to make it through this experience. We would check all her wires, get her a sip of ice water and check all the computer readings at every little noise she would make.

The ICU nurses were fantastic. They made each patient a beautiful blanket, and we placed Ella's over her to keep her warm. She made it through that first night; and so did we.

I slept on a cot beside Ella for the next five days in the hospital. I watched them make her stand the first morning after surgery - it made me hurt!

There were ups and downs in her recovery, but every day Ella got stronger and brighter and her wonderful smile was coming back. The golden retriever who came by each day to help her forget why she was there always brought a smile. Her frown returned when the physical therapist would arrive to bring more pain to Ella!

It was a huge victory on the fourth day that we could walk all the way around the nurses' station - Ella and her IV!! She could now thank her physical therapist with a smile.

It was finally time to bring her back home - and now I was nervous again. She was still pretty fragile and had a lot of pain. Every bump in the car ride sent her wailing. My husband couldn't drive smoothly enough! What would we do without all those wonderful nurses checking on Ella?

Every day brought new challenges and new strength.

Her amazing body had tried since birth to try to fix itself. It had built a shelf of bone that hid the fact that her sacrum was not connected to her L5 - thus the butt pain. The decompression treatment had torn the ligaments that were holding it in place. The doctor had to chip away all that bone shelf that was in the way and place rods from the sacrum to the L5 to fix it.

It's always the 20/20 vision after the fact, but had she not had the terrible experience with the decompression treatment we might not have found the real problem of much of her pain. So I have learned that through every terrible experience there is always a silver lining if we are patient enough to find it. We have all learned how to breathe through the pain, accept what is before us and become stronger for what comes next. God granted our prayers and for that we will always be eternally grateful.

Pause, breathe, let go of what you can't change, that was my mind set. In the midst of all the chaos we tried to stay centered on what was best for Ella.

Ella had another mind set - "never quit." She wanted to ride again. She wanted to compete again. We met halfway with the doctor's orders. She rode our most trustworthy horse, CD, but had to give up contact sports.

That left running. She began running cross country and track in her sophomore year and struggled. But with every passing year, she kept pounding away working on her core and her overall strength. Ella became a valuable runner in both sports going to regionals and performing well her junior and senior year in high school.

After graduation she still had the desire to run. Staying home to attend Junior College, she was inspired to continue running. The very first race, The Barefoot 5K, she won in 18:33! Her goal was the San Antonio Rock 'n Roll half marathon, which she completed in an incredible time of 1:36.

This love of running, her success every time she ran and her desire to keep pushing herself to new limits led her to a wonderful opportunity to compete in obstacle running.

All this success also brought her interest from sponsors. That is all exciting, but it can also be a worry. Too much pressure to be perfect - difficult race schedules - having to make a lot of people happy. I felt like sometimes Ella forgot what really made her happy.

Ella has endured several injuries while competing over the last several years, but she is not a quitter. Ella continues to train. She continues to be a strong person with a giving heart. She has unprecedented empathy for those who suffer from physical ailments and serves as an inspiration for many to never quit on themselves. She is a living example that anything is possible if you have courage, determination and true grit! As Vince Lombardi would say, "never quit." Ella has dreams and with her courageous attitude she will be a success at whatever she chooses.

Lucky are all of us whose lives she has touched.

CHAPTER 3
CREATION

The development of a mad woman.

Love thy flaws. Love thy perfections.

I will soon discover myself finding peace in the dark hours of the gym with beads of sweat rolling down my brow line, however, I am too concentrated on finishing my set that I do not stop to wipe away my sweat.

The exhausting stiffness of blood flowing through my muscles brought me a slight smirk and I didn't want to stop. I enjoyed the pain, the silent suffering, the chance to break a barrier. More importantly, I enjoyed being able to feel alive, knowing that there was a breaking point somewhere near.

I am breakable, and I like it, but I also like the fact that I feel otherwise.

When I first started training I was uncertain of what I was actually doing but I did it with confidence. I entered the gym with my short spandex hugging my body, my shirt's sleeves were cut and tucked underneath my sports bra and my headphones were already in my ears blaring music, obviously way too loud.

My 'don't talk to me' face was engaged and I headed straight to the dumbbells. As I reached over to pick up the weights I observed my arms and their definition contract with the heaviness of the iron in my hands. I fell in love with the progress I saw day in and day out, whether that change was just microscopic or not.

I could feel the growth inside me as my obsession with my body image grew in an unhealthy manner.

Any meathead will agree with me, that the feeling of the pump is addictive. It is sinfully delicious and I always crave its accustomed ache. It hurts so good but also at the same time makes you feel so alive. Like a starving lion, I thrive off of it. I am the King of this land and it is a necessity for me to have it. But unlike the big feline, I don't make my bitches get my dinner, I hunt it down, I do the work.

Sure, you could say I became extremely obsessed with working out but I never truly had the privilege of having a body that could handle intentional pain and growth and now that I had the ability to do so, I fell head over heels for the pump.

Being able to induce self-labor and work on oneself is a privilege we must learn to appreciate and not take for granted.

Give me torn muscle fibers, I like that shit.

I sincerely take pleasure in the chronic tiredness you experience after a hard training session, it lingers with you for the remainder of the day, leaving you to waddle around and strain to get up, postponing bathroom breaks until the very last second.

Pissed my pants.

However, due to my back condition I was, and still am, terribly inconsistent. There are days when I would wake up and my back needs to be stretched for thirty minutes before I can even begin to function right. I have to sleep with a pillow in between my legs at night or I'll wake up with too much of an ache. I can hardly wear shoes that don't have support. Sitting or standing for long periods of time will upset it, even bending over slightly or doing simple movements will set it off. It's also not always strong enough to withstand back squats or deadlifts, so for the longest time I did bodyweight squats in between each set even if it was chest day. I had to learn how to train around my spine and in order to make myself stronger I knew that if I built up my hamstrings along with my core, my lower back would get better.

Ask anyone who knows me, I will be under the squat rack for hours doing front squats, back squats, box squats, training them heavy, tempo, high volume, doing drop sets, supersets, I will literally train my legs until I puke or fall down.

It's as if I remember the times when I couldn't walk.

At the time, my obsession with training felt normal. It was an easy way for me to get a release from all the tension bottled up inside. Even nowadays it still has the same benefits.

I had constant anger, sadness, frustration, and a confusion that controlled me. Therefore my solution to control such abusive emotions was to drop the hammer on my own self through weight lifting and running just to find some sort of peace.

Honestly, I felt invisible in the gym or even out on the trails. Inside my head I knew what I had overcome just to be able to put one foot in front of the other and that gave me an undeniable edge on adversity.

Bring it.

It made me grit my teeth when I heard others complain about their small issues in their simple little lives and with that I grew slightly bitter with the idea of wasting a moment. I was on a mission to find that balance between sanity and insanity because it was there on that beam where I could truly be myself. I wanted to walk that beam so badly that even if it meant I had to risk my everything for the chance to do something great with my life, I was going to do it. It made me feel absolutely crazy.

In college, I spent my entire time planning my life out. During algebra I wrote up training programs, workouts, organized my meal plans, my sets, and the miles I needed to hit while my teacher explained how x divided by purple bananas equals muffin sauce. Math confused me, school worried me, I didn't find any interest in its labors and I attended it because that's what society told me to do.

The only subject that I truly cared for was psychology. In those classes, I would finally push aside my training notebooks, turn the gears in my head off and listen to how the brain works, partly because I knew that mine was different.

Often I found myself self-diagnosing through its teachings. For example, according to Erik Erikson's stages of psychosocial development, in stage five adolescence, teens go through "identity versus confusion" where we explore different behaviors, personalities, and roles. Those who achieve a good sense of self and a strong identity will accomplish control and their own personal independence. However, those who fail to achieve this will feel lost and insecure.

After stage five, we go to stage six where we face intimacy versus isolation. It states that if one has a poor sense of self or lacks to acknowledge it, they will have intimacy issues and seek isolation. Studies have shown that individuals who do not have a good sense of self are more likely to struggle with emotional isolation, depression, and loneliness.

I'd think to myself, "I don't know who I am."

But everyone around me seemed to know me.

Greatness is an ache in your soul.
You have to want it so badly, it hurts.

It was my cancer and it instantaneously infected my lungs, my brain, and my heart and you know what? I wanted this infectious disease to spread throughout me and I wanted to be caught chuckling in frustration with my misunderstood desires because, after all, I was a monster created by all things negative.

These shadows were friendly to me and I viewed the breakdowns they brought to me in a positive light, now while my outlook on life appeared to be incredibly twisted and tainted, my intentions were full of good even though I sure as hell didn't feel all that good sometimes.

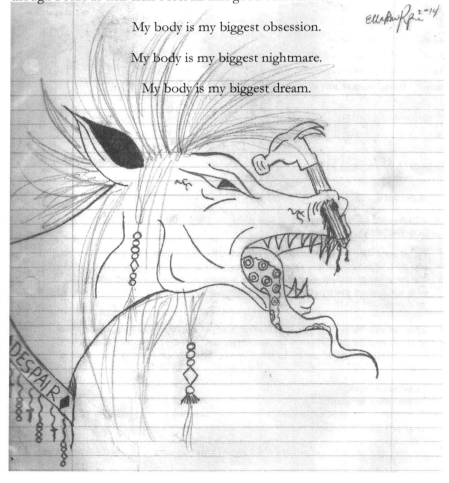

My body is my biggest obsession.

My body is my biggest nightmare.

My body is my biggest dream.

Easily one of the saddest things about success is the loss of friendships that can come with it. Fame isn't all rainbows and cotton candy, more like fake unicorns and dog shit with the occasional participation ribbon handed out… And yeah, I said fake unicorns.

As unfortunate as it was, my closest friend and I 'split up' and our friendship became tainted and altered just like you see in the movies. She grew distant from my reach and I began to draw back my finger tips from her direction. It became quite clear we were no longer friends and this saddened me greatly for it felt like a random attack.

I sulked more into my lonesome life and moved onward. It sucked, it really, really did, I don't know whether it was my fault or not, but losing a best friend over something that you love sucks. Especially if that something is healthy, rewarding, and beneficial in all the right ways for you.

Sometimes when you find something that you're good at, your good friends become not so good.

I grew a nasty, bitter taste towards you, mainly because I hated seeing your back when I reached so far out for you. Even more than that, I hated the fact that you questioned my passion and labeled me 'different' once I hit success, even after knowing me for so long. It got so sour for me, that even the whisper of your name spiked the hair on the back of my neck to stand. I felt an overwhelming sensation, an aggressive decision to disconnect myself from you, and so I did.

Forever alone.

My love life was no different. While I was young and busy at this point in my life, I saw members of the opposite sex pause to watch me walk across the gym floor. I saw their eyes attract to my legs, my hair, my arms, yet I stayed away from them because all I saw in them was a distraction.

I developed intimacy issues due to the hidden reality that I did not love myself and therefore I could not love someone else.

I didn't want to expose my body to anyone. Just the thought of my body naked and that vulnerable to be judged intimidated me. So I hid it from others.

Nor did I even dare to want to be touched either, I veered away from peoples' hands as they reached out to tickle, poke, or sometimes even hug me.

Please, don't feel me too much.

I hated it when people requested to see my 'ripped' stomach. Even though I'm a tight, hundred and twenty pound girl lifting thirty-five pounds on the shoulder press, I'm just not good enough yet. I need to be leaner.

When asked on dates, I rejected them with lame excuses or simply just ignored their calls or texts. When asked about my sex life, I laughed. What sex life? What relationships are you talking about?

Everyone who seemed to approach me ended up becoming an annoyance, with their superficial muscles, their lack of intelligence and lack of actual care for others. They all seemed to be trying to be something they weren't. Shit, even I was trying to be a 120 pound athlete and that simply wasn't me.

<u>2006: The start of it all.</u>

I can recall the majority of my classmates complaining about their backs bothering them and that doing an overhead volleyball serve was going to be the death of them.

"Can you overhead serve yet?"

"No, it hurts my back."

"You won't get on A team if you can only underhand it."

"Girl, I know."

Seventh grade. That precious time when the opposite sex is suddenly new and attractive, when it actually really does matter where and who you sit with at lunch, and when we learn to judge others by their appearances and fitting in is the cool thing to do.

Finally I'm old enough for athletics and of course, I compete in all the sports my school has to offer me, except golf and tennis.

I always had a weird feeling in my back but just never really thought much of it. It was like an annoying gnat, just buzzing slightly in my head.

"Hey, hey, hey, oh hi there."

When volleyball season came along, early in the school year, everyone began to complain about how the overhead serve made their back hurt.

Oh, everyone else has an annoying gnat too. Hi.

A couple of weeks into volleyball season and the coaches started to notice my posture failing me, that I could not seem to stand properly, and the gradual loss of function in my legs. My back gave out on me occasionally which caused me to dramatically collapse onto the court.

My classmates would laugh at me, point their fingers as they made fun of me while I fell to the ground. I was called 'out of control' and at the time it was all silly jokes until my big, misunderstood situation became terrifyingly serious after my horse riding accident.

I didn't attend middle school very much, I was found mainly at home cuddling my stuffed animals. I drowned in Vicodin and muscle relaxers just to make it through my day, only to fade away into an achy sleep for hours, then to awaken and repeat the same misery all over again.

Even if I did have the strength to go to school, I wandered around in a heavy haze, carrying a pillow around with me because I could not stand the feeling of the hard chairs against my back and buttocks, I became known as 'the girl with the pillow' and I hated that shit.

"Hey Ella, where's your pillow?"

"Shut up."

I had my surgery in my eighth grade year, in 2007, when I was thirteen years young and I spent the next few months in serious rehab until my freshman year of high school.

Entering high school I was optimistic about returning to athletics and starting over, even though I still attended physical therapy. But of course, I wasn't ready for any of it, even though I believed I was.

I tried out for basketball even though I was told I could not do any contact sports and just as expected, my body failed me. It only caused me more mental stress and pain to have to quit. It was hard for me to accept, but I finally came to terms with the fact that my spine wasn't healthy yet. So I spent the remainder of my year on the sidelines.

My sophomore year came, and I began to run. I also began to ride my horse more and, with the positive reinforcement from my parents, I tried out for cross country and track. Sure enough, I made the teams.

Slowly but surely, I progressed forward against my rigid odds.

However, like most young kids in high school I began to experiment with underage drinking in my sophomore year. I found that drinking was an easy way to put up a protective wall against my internal sadness. I could lose control while being in control.

It was my first glimpse at what it was like inside my head. It was also a glimpse at the first signs of having a mental disorder because I found terrifying thoughts of being unworthy.

Through that cheap beer and liquor, I heard my demons for the first time.

"HEY ELLA HOW ARE YOU DOING? NOT GOING TO BE SO WELL ANYMORE."

A strange sadness crept into my soul, and so with those voices echoing throughout my head, I started to drink just about every weekend. I got cross-faded just so I could blend my days away with the wrong kinds of people.

I went through phases of wearing dark makeup like every typical troubled kid goes through. I cut my hair into a shag, dressed as if I was a hippie with headbands around my forehead. To me it was all normal, it was just me expressing how lost I was. No one knew it at the time or could even tell, hell I didn't even really know it, but I was sad as hell.

By the end of my junior year, I quit partying and being a brat cold turkey to focus on being a healthier Ella and I began to work harder by the day in regards to my fitness level.

I got faster, and soon my weirdness became attractive to others. It was an awesome spoonful of belief being fed to my ego. I can do this… Delicious!

However becoming healthy and fit wasn't easy for me. Most of my workouts in high school ended with me bent over grabbing my back, in tears due to the crippling pain emerging throughout my body. The pounding of running caused sporadic muscle cramps, many of my nerves got pinched by the metal rods, and the lack of muscle and strength alone in my back was difficult to deal with.

My body was an annoying strain for me to get used to. It simply couldn't keep up with my mind and that was one of the hardest things to accept. But I took it. I took it pretty lightly, but hell, I took it as it came. And it wasn't so light.

While running cross country and track, I wasn't the best on the team but I sure as hell gave it my best throughout my junior and senior year. Each year I was rewarded the heart award for my efforts. I made it as far as regionals with my teams in both track and cross country and it was enough to light a spark inside me. Perhaps I could do something physical with my life.

So I kept on running and I most definitely kept on riding my horses. It didn't take long for me to get back into the endurance world and I began to enter into many twenty-five mile and fifty mile horse races, placing well with my new horse Chance.

Socks lived to be thirty two years old and I retired her from racing at the age of twenty-seven. She was one stubborn horse right until death, and I admired her more than I could ever admire some fitness model in a magazine. Socks was a fighter.

As she became old, her health deteriorated and she lost majority of her teeth which caused her to lose a lot of weight very quickly. She would colic often, we found her isolating herself from the other horses so that she could linger in the pasture alone.

It became obvious to me that my horse was dying of old age. More than that, she was suffering. I realized and accepted that it was in my hands to play the role of God, so in the attempt to help her find peace we put her down before she either starved herself to death or died due to colicing.

Walking her to the stall at the vet's that warm morning was one incredibly gut wrenching moment that I wasn't ready for. But I believe that Socks was ready to go onto her next chapter in life.

I stood there crying next to her in the stall as her head nudged into the crease of my arms, her long nose whiskers tickling my biceps as I ran my hands down her once strong neck. Her coat still maintained a silky feel.

Baby girl, you were the best and I'll miss you. I kissed her forehead and we parted ways.

I purchased Chance a few months after the passing of Socks and he was another horse who had been beaten and left trembling at the sight of a whip. But there was just something about the darkness he possessed that attracted me. I wanted to help him.

Maybe it was because I shared the darkness he felt.

All you really need in life is a chance and he was mine. That may sound cheesy and a bit dorky, but it was a simple truth that we could not deny even if we wanted to.

Chance is a dark blood bay, young Russian Arabian gelding standing at 15.1 hands with little to no markings except one white back foot. He is a beautiful athlete but he sure had been messed with one too many times and we quickly learned that he wouldn't take shit from anyone.

Upon getting him, my mother and I were unaware of just how damaged the horse was until we asked him to enter a trailer. He freaked out, broke the divider door, reared, kicked out, snarled his teeth, and refused to obey our coaxing methods.

He seemed to hate everyone, especially if they were of the male sex and if you had a blanket… Oh man, good luck with that.

He would pin his ears back at you, he kicked his back feet out in a fury, and backed up into your torso anytime you entered his stall. The horse was a damn monster and I found myself crying many times in my attempts to help him.

"What did they do to you poor boy?"

But in time, I found out that he loved soft peppermints, that he really just wanted to be loved but didn't know how to accept it, and that this horse was another chance for me to learn more about life and even about myself.

It took a solid year of hard, patient work for Chance to finally accept my love and it paid off. He soon began to follow me around in the pasture like a puppy dog, he started to enter the trailer willingly, he eventually accepted the warmth of a blanket on his back, and nudged his head into my hair to play with me instead of threatening me with his backend.

I saw the change in him and we began to compete more regularly, placing top ten in most of our twenty-five mile races; we even competed in a couple of fifty milers.

Chance was a prime example that despite having such great negatives in your life, you can become positive… He showed that all you need is a chance to make that change, and that you need to start believing in yourself, even if you think that you cannot possibly be something great.

Content.

It wasn't until after high school that I really got the desire to become something great physically, mentally, spiritually, and emotionally. It settled into my head that my second chance to be something great was actually something real and that I really was special enough to change the world.

Let's change the world.

Let's be a beacon.

Success came fast to me, almost too fast at that, and I often found myself overwhelmed. Even though I was terribly unaware of the pressures of this success at first, they eventually began to weigh me down. What a heavy, heavy blanket I had draped around my shoulders. Without thinking too much about it, I believed that I was handling it maturely but it became quite clear later on in my life that success isn't just what made me, it also broke me.

By the time I was eighteen years young I was already sponsored by a few small companies and flying across America to compete in obstacle races, mainly in the Spartan Race series. When I was nineteen I signed an even bigger contract with Reebok Spartan Race. Then when I turned twenty I signed with MHP Supplements.

Like I said, success came very fast. I didn't know if I was ready for its rotten exposures and heavy pressures but it came at me with a vengeance.

Fall on your face Ella Anne.

In the very beginning of my trek to become something great I got caught up in chaos of diets, training fads, methods, myths, social pressures, the straight bullshit being told by so many 'gurus', and all that other fitness nonsense out there. Oh how it took a hold of me, a nasty hold that just about ruined my life.

Eat this, not that. Train like this, not like that.

Before I knew it, my life became obsessively restricted and even more isolated than it was before. I was in the gym at five in morning running mile repeats, followed by an entire body workout that lasted up to ninety minutes. This entire workout was performed fasted.

The remainder of my day was a window of 500-600 calories while pumping my body with caffeine just to make it through the day, then back to the gym in the evening after classes to train weights, again.

After training I'd come home, skip dinner or surgically slice up my food into small pieces so that I would only take small bites. Even the tiny amount of food that I'd consume made me feel fat.

Before my brain took over and I could realize just how hungry I was, I would run upstairs and make sure to be in my bed by eight o'clock just about every night.

I didn't seem to mind the loneliness, that was just my lifestyle, it was a lifestyle that I blindly lived and it didn't even occur to me that I had an issue until I began to become so malnourished that eventually I stop practicing anorexia and became bulimic.

I am an extremist at heart, but my heart is incredibly broken.

I started to live off of the feeling of being hungry and forgot what it was like to be full. If I ever dared to allow myself to eat something that even remotely filled me up, I felt sick; I hated how my stomach would feel with all this food in my body. The only real full feeling I felt during this time was the bloat from the carbonation of diet sodas, loads of water, coffee, and raw or steamed vegetables.

Feeling hungry was a benchmark of my progress and it overlooked my success; it informed me that I was on the right path.

Now don't get me wrong here, I would still eat *some* food, not a lot of food, but it was just enough to get by. Everything I ate was labeled with its nutrition facts so I knew exactly what I was eating. It was either 'sugar free' or 'fat free', or I cooked it myself so that I would know that it was not prepped in oil or salt.

Every morning I rolled out of bed feeling hungry, my mouth dry, my back stiff, and feeling overly fatigued but all that was normal for me. Rubbing my eyes like a little kid does, hair looking like a messy mop, I would make my way over to my mirror with my shirt lifted up to my chest so I could glare at my abdominals.

"How they lookin'?"

I'd spend hours examining myself, judging and trying to figure out if I got leaner, if I was more ripped than the day before, if I got fat from that extra bite of chicken I ate the previous night.

"Am I fat? YOU'RE FAT!"

Even though I was thin I hated wearing tight clothing, I didn't want anything to be touching the tissue on my stomach; it was forever sacred. Unfortunately, from that time on, I have carried this feeling with me in my life and I will never fully appreciate a belly rub like I once did when I was a little kid.

For the amount of training I was doing I should have been eating anywhere from 2,000 to 3,500 calories. Obviously this depends on my metabolism and a few other factors, but regardless of that, I was still a ridiculous amount under than what I should have been eating.

I was running anywhere from fifty-five to seventy miles a week, lifting weights six times a week, and just about every weekend I was off doing some kind of race, either a horse race, road race, or obstacle race.

I was on the go.

My goal was to eat around five hundred calories a day. Some days I ate seven hundred or more and hated myself for it. Occasionally I had days where I had no carbs or fats, other days I ate little to nothing but some protein shakes, and every day I made sure that the amount of calories I burned while doing the stairs, bike, or row machine matched the calories that I ate.

My first competition goal upon graduating high school, in November 2011, was to run a half marathon. It was a crazy thought to me. I hated running anything over two hundred meters, so thirteen miles seemed ridiculous. I am a sprinter, I don't do endurance. Ah-haha, but I sure do love a challenge, so I went after it. Long distance simply sucked to me but once I decide to do something, I lock my head and heart on it, it's all or nothing. So I began to run every day before class and lift weights in the evening.

In high school I was always a bit thick but never really fat. My legs and butt were bigger than most, my stomach was flat but not with rippling muscle, and my arms didn't jiggle, I was a healthy teenage girl.

During my prep for this half marathon is when I began practicing the behaviors of an anorexic. I became scrawny, my big legs and butt disappeared, my stomach flattened out enough that my abdominals showed only due to starvation, and my arms were sticks with just enough muscle on them to get me through my workouts. I lived off little to no food all day while extensively exercising. That was it; that was how I started my career, my life.

I am partly successful due to my failures, don't you forget that, I didn't become successful in a healthy way.

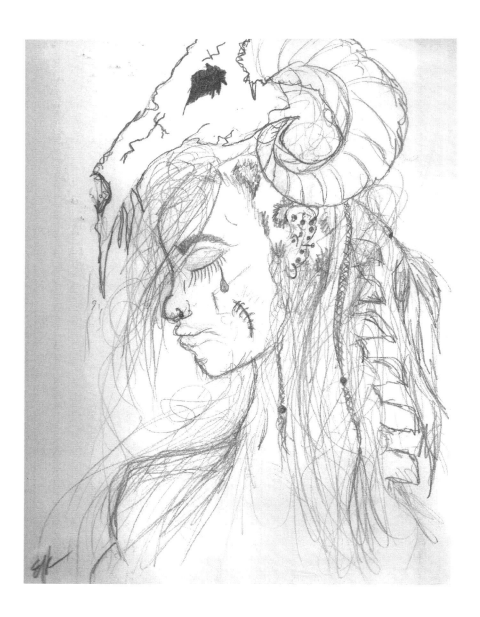

I spent the evening before my half marathon with a friend down at the river walk in San Antonio, Texas. As she ordered a huge plate of fajitas, I felt my teeth bite my lips, I wanted food, I wanted lots of food. I felt safe enough to allow myself to get a big plate of enchiladas, rice, beans, and grilled vegetables in front of her.

Well this was weird.

Before I knew it, I was plowing through my entire plate of food within a few seconds, not once did I set my fork down.

"I must hurry, I might not get this chance again to have food like this in front of me."

Immediately after eating everything, I finally felt it all, the guilt, the confusion, the frustration, the aches.

"What have I just done?"

When we got back to my brother's place, I tried to go to the restroom to throw it all up. I turned the faucet on to try to drown out my gagging noises as I knelt down in front of the toilet with my left hand ready. I was crying quietly to myself as I forced my fingers into my mouth, my eyes pierced through the ceiling, hating myself for doing this but I had to get rid of it.

I tried hard to get all of it out of me but found myself making too much noise, so I stopped. I didn't want to get caught, not here, not now. So I stopped and looked at myself in the mirror. My reflection showed my red eyes, my swollen, running nose, and the sick combination of refried beans and chicken enchilada vile on my lips. I quickly smeared it all off and splashed water onto my face.

Wash away my sins. This didn't just happen. I don't have a problem.

The next morning I ran the half marathon with a destroyed stomach that caused me to stop at mile four for about five minutes of pure agony. And about half a mile from the finish line, one of my metal rods pinched my sciatic nerve.

At an hour and thirty-six minutes, I ran across the timing mat with tears running down my face, my left leg numb, my stomach in knots, and my back screeching in pain.

I finished my first goal sobbing.

I cried for many reasons, I cried because my back would forever hinder me in ways I could not control, it was a constant reminder that I was not normal, and I cried because of the guilt from yesterday's binge. The memory of the attempts to puke in my brother's house still weighed heavy in my heart.

My half marathon was just a few weeks before Thanksgiving and it ended up being one of the saddest family gatherings I have ever had. With the extra time off from school, I found myself having more time to chow down aimlessly as I anxiously awaited the day of feasting. I knew what was coming for me, I was going to lose absolute control and it was frightening the hell out of me.

On Thanksgiving day, my family and I splurged into my mother's amazing dishes of sweet potato and black bean hash, glazed turkey, stuffing, buttery mashed potatoes, pumpkin pie, homemade apple pie, and all of the other wonderful holiday foods.

I ate and oh boy did I eat.

I ate so much that my stomach soon resembled a beer belly. But that didn't stop me. I kept eating past my limits, I could not stop. When I tried to stop I looked over at my family, I watched as my brothers ate, I watched as my sister hardly ate, and I watched as my mother and father smiled amongst us.

"Why do I feel so sad inside and why can't I stop eating?"

I went to the restroom in between each plate full of food to puke my brains out. After doing so, I cried for a few minutes, questioning myself as I wiped away my tears, washed my face and went back to the dinner table to put on a fake smile, oh the holidays.

Thanksgiving in 2011 made me hate the holidays because inside I was trembling. I was hating my household because everywhere I seemed to look, there was temptation. There was also happiness all around me but I could not feel it.

My demons were laughing at me, grabbing my throat.

"You're ours Ella Anne, you're so weak, you need us."

It was driving me insane and controlling my head, making me do such painful things to myself. I didn't want to do any of it, but it was literally my loss of sanity that brought me to such low levels.

After most of my binges I would attempt to go to the gym to even out my sins. I'd wear hoodies with my bloodshot eyes looking down to the floor avoiding eye contact, the constant heartburn pulsing through my throat with each step I take.

I trained until I couldn't stand anymore, until I dropped to the floor. It didn't even matter if anyone else was in the gym, I was there destroying my only friend.

My body couldn't keep up with my mind and without even trying to hide it, I vomited everywhere, fell to my knees, and cried. As I hammered myself down to the ground, I wanted so badly to get away.

I wanted so badly to be great that it hurts me. I would never get there like this.

Emotionally I was exhausted, but that was just another little obstacle for me to conquer. So there I was in my sweats slaying through all the supersets, drop sets, and dumb amounts of cardio that I did for hours. It seemed that by doing this that I could find some sort of peace with my actions and mask over my mistakes.

A rise and a fall was all I could bear to do, it evened the playing field. But really, my eating disorder is winning, I was losing this game.

I'm a loser. Hey.

Speaking of losing, not once did I place lower than third while I was 'healthy' to compete. I literally was a freak. Let me brag for a second, the only times where I placed lower than podium was if I was injured or got injured during a race which started to become more frequent later on in my career due to my health issues.

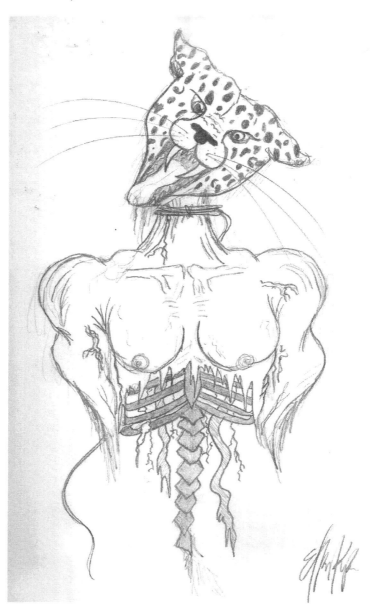

The first time I ever forced myself to puke after a meal was about a month before I did my half marathon, and I made sure to write it down in my journal. I didn't have any friends that I knew of who were bulimic or anorexic. I didn't read books about those who practice purging their food. Nobody even told me to throw my food up so that I could get rid of it, I just did it.

All I knew is that I needed to get rid of it, to clean myself of all this pain that lived inside me and the only way to do that was to impose more pain into my life.

Stick my fingers down my throat, it was that simple, get rid of it all, it'll all be gone, I'll be like new again.

Who is Ella Anne Kociuba?

I can remember crying so hard and feeling so confused as to why I had just done what I did. I thought "I'll never do it again, it's a one-time thing. Now I know what that's like, I'll never do it again, that was dumb."

Of course I told myself this nonsense bullshit during the hype of my curiosity with self-abuse but I knew deep down that after that incident, I'd never be the same, I'd be lost in my head for what would feel like forever.

75

On one weekend in the fall, my mother and I traveled to Cat Springs, Texas to compete in a twenty five mile horse race together.

Competing in endurance races was a graceful escape for me, it was my true happy place where I could get away from the world to go and enjoy a beautiful, foreign land with just my horse. But now that bulimia has got a hold of me, it's not so beautiful anymore, nothing really is.

Usually in these races, Chance and I would end up pulling away from Cocoa and her to finish in the top ten.

Unfortunately, I ended up binging on all the food that we had stored in the cooler and anxiously started to await my chance to get rid of it. The jitters hit me suddenly, so I paced around with my hands touching my face, trying so hard to resist it, my heart was pulsing out of my chest and my head was spinning. I just had to sneak away so I could throw it all up, I needed an escape. Luckily my mother went for a quick walk to check out the showers. That was my chance, and so I went behind the trailer to secretly stick my fingers down my throat and threw up everything.

"What am I doing with my life?"

Once I finished puking until there was nothing left, I looked over at Chance grazing on his hay, his dark coat shining brightly, showing his athleticism, his finely dished face popping up to the sounds of other horse's neighing in the distance. He scans the earth with such innocence as I looked at him with such guilt.

I was hunched over with my fingers dripping with thick vomit and stomach acid, tears were streaming down my face, my hair blew in the light wind, and the dry grass stabbed me through my tights, I wanted to die sometimes.

As odd as it was, shortly after becoming bulimic, suddenly success really started to come towards me, knocking at my doors.

"Hey Ella! Whatchya doin' there? Wanna breakdown for me?"

And maybe, just maybe, I thought to myself, I was doing something right, that this was right. HA! Whatever! I fully doubted it. I knew that it was a problem but not once did I stop for long to think about it or on how to fix it. I just suppressed the hell out of it.

These memories, oh these memories, let's just make them go away by acting like it didn't ever happen.

"I never did any of that nonsense, duh! That's for weak minded individuals and I'm strong, I'm Ella Anne Kociuba!"

"Oh but Ella, don't you know that you can't fool yourself for too long, this isn't about being a weak or strong minded individual, we all know what you're capable of. This disorder is about something much greater than that."

Letting go.

I was fully aware of the damages that bulimia and anorexia do to your body. I was extremely educated on nutrition through my own research, and I even gave advice to others about how to avoid falling into bad eating habits, but I was already too sick in the head to listen to my own words.

Sometimes I even bad mouthed those who were struggling with eating disorders, I believed they couldn't get their shit together, that they were weak.

HA! Oh how I would eventually end up swallowing and throwing up those words!

Foolish I once was.

Sometimes I wonder what my life would be like if I hadn't fallen into an eating disorder as my go to. Would if I had veered towards using heavy drugs or to cutting myself? What if I hadn't had an eating disorder at all? What would life be like then?

That shit, I'll never know.

A few times I binged due to the emotional surges of feeling off, something going wrong in my day. Even if it was as simple as having my debit card declined because I had no money, or waking up a few minutes late. If someone said something rude to me, or I got in a fight with my parents or a friend, I heard the hunger. But those made up only about ten percent of the reasons. The other ninety percent of the time I had no idea why I did what I did, why the voice was there, and why I found myself in front of the toilet dangling my fingers down my throat.

"Please be quiet, please get out of me."

Constantly, there was this voice inside me, this hunger even when I wasn't hungry.

"Eat Ella!"

There was this ache, this uncontrollable monster wanting to play even when I was tired.

"Let's go explore Ella!"

I would just let it have its way.

I was afraid of myself.

At the end of 2011 through to the beginning of 2012, when I was just eighteen years young, I felt as if the world was my playground, I jumped through its creek beds, ran around its broken paths, and climbed up its rocky hills.

"This is all mine!" I thought to myself "I'm going to be great. I am eighteen and I can see my own potential inside me everywhere I look and boy does it look great!"

My back pain was finally decreasing by the day as I hammered intentional pain into myself. It was the simple expression of being able to induce adversity upon myself that caused me to topple over the chronic pain that already lived within me. With that I began to devour adversity like it was cake. It was the shit I needed to live!

"Feed me, feed me, I'm so hungry and I'm so selfish, give me everything, take everything from me."

For the longest time I feared food, I worried about every little bite that I took because I would gain fat from it, my muscles would also become soft and I praised the days where I fasted or had burned an equal amount of calories in the gym.

I was anorexic and I didn't even know it until a couple years later when I started to write this book.

Some of my friends looked at me with curious eyes questioning my lifestyle.

"Don't you dare look at me like that! I AM HEALTHY! Can someone say denial? ME! I CAN! Denial, denial, denial.

My friends: "You're so skinny."

Me: "No I'm not. I'm not shredded enough."

My friends: "What are you even eating?"

Me: "I eat all the time! You kidding me?"

My friends: "I wish I had your abs!"

Me: "What abs?"

I was so blind and ashamed about my body, I was never good enough in my own eyes and that sickens me as I write it now.

I didn't want to be viewed as 'that weak girl who has an eating disorder', that's so unattractive. "I'm a strong athlete", I tell myself, "I got this". Look at me. I overcame my back injury, I win all these races, I have a following, I'm big time so no one can ever see me like this." Ever was the keyword here.

I kept telling myself "I'm Ella Kociuba, people can't know this, people can't see this side of me, I'm strong, I got this, this is nothing, I'm in control."

I didn't want to give up my precious body and my insane habits because regardless of the damages they caused, I was becoming "successful" from them.

Starting off, my diet was extremely restricted, I consumed only: egg whites, old-fashioned oatmeal with no cream or milk, organic peanut butter, white fish that was baked in the oven, grilled chicken with either no seasoning, or salt-free seasonings, sweet potatoes with nothing on them, brown rice, steamed vegetables like asparagus, broccoli, and spinach, and fat-free Greek yogurt.

I ate six times a day every three hours, on the hour, no minute later, no minute sooner and I made sure to have all my meals in Tupperware as I went to school, hung out with friends, and even when I went out to go shopping. I never skipped one of my plain-ass meals.

If I happened to 'slip up' on my diet and eat anything that wasn't on that list, like white rice, chicken that had oil on it, buttered potatoes, an extra tablespoon of peanut butter, a potato chip, or a candy bar, I immediately threw down the towel and said, "FUCK IT, YOU OBVIOUSLY DON'T WANT IT BAD ENOUGH, YOU'RE JUST A PIG!"

I told myself I wasn't dedicated enough, I didn't want this bad enough, I wasn't even making enough sacrifices, I was weak, I was just full of such excuses, and so I would end up binging on whatever was around me.

It was like a religion. I went there to find comfort, deliver my body over to it, and listen to its verses without ever fully understanding them. I went there because it was what I'd been doing for a while now and it was just easy to blindly follow its teachings and demands.

Deliver me.

So I did as so many others had done before me. I got down onto my knees and prayed for something I could not seem to find. I needed it, I didn't need it. I devoured its offerings. These were the ways. It was what I believed in. How dare I go outside its holy doors? Forgive me. This religion I praised was more of a twisted cult and it was running me straight into the ground because I was never going to be good enough for it.

You see it everywhere you go: "Lose fifteen pounds in two weeks!", "Get a flat tummy in less than a month!" This generation is fixated on our bodies, on our materials, and on our ungrateful lifestyles that we don't even embrace, we just go through the motions.

We live day to day looking at magazines, books, and hearing TV programs, and the news talk about how so-and-so gained weight, how you can lose weight with this new diet pill, that eating complex carbs only is the way to go, that this new product will get rid of your cellulite.

It's brain washing us to believe we're never good enough.

We live in such bullshit that it's really not much of a surprise that about twenty-four million people suffer form an eating disorder.

You also hear it at the gym, restaurants, at your friend's house, from your parents, in the grocery store, at church.

"Oh I really shouldn't go out to eat, I'm trying to lose weight," "I shouldn't have breakfast because I ate so much last night," "I can't be a size two if I eat a piece of that cake." Then there's the best one: "I feel fat today so I'm going to fast."

It's just floating around us like an obnoxious cigarette that is lit in a smoke free zone. We are all getting second-hand smoke here whether we realize it or not. It is brainwashing us to believe that if we starve ourselves, if we skip meals, if we bash on our bodies, that we are normal. We are normal for doing these things, it is popular, it is what the world talks about constantly.

So go ahead, skip your breakfast, eat no gluten, have no carbs after six in the afternoon, and get plastic surgery to get rid of your imperfections. That shit is normal. Our surroundings and our brains tell us so.

It's okay, we're all fucked up.

I began to get lost in this obsession with greatness and it was in these moments of pure fascination where I decided to sketch myself, even though all my lines were skewed.

Shortly after running my first ever Spartan Race in December of 2011, I ended up tearing some ligaments in my knee that had me in tears on the sidelines.

"I can't run! What do I do?"

So I decided to strip down and be almost naked in a tiny suit, put on an obnoxious fake tan, fix my hair, plaster my eyes with makeup and flex my depleted muscles on a stage. Yeah, that's right, I did a bodybuilding show where I competed in both figure and bikini.

It just seemed like the right thing to do for me. Since my knee was a bum and I had this burning passion for competing, I had to do something, so focusing on building more muscle and doing a show would hand-feed me my poison since I couldn't do any obstacle races.

The hard definition of muscled bodies appearing like a biology book walking around with so many googley eyes watching them, was brutally attractive to me. It was all so intriguing, the dedication, the science behind it, the training, the nutrition. I wanted to have this foreign thing called 'physical strength' for myself and I wanted to be what they called 'shredded'.

So my diet got even stricter, I started to starve myself more. I made even bigger slip-ups on my diet, beat myself up more mentally, and slaved through more hours in the gym. I became so intoxicated with this impossible image of what greatness was that I became completely blind to everything else.

"I must lean down for this show, I need my abs to pop more, I need my shoulders to cap off, I want the tear drops in my quads to start sobbing for all to see, and I want my ass to be perky and tight."

My body was my biggest obsession. The extremist within me raged.

"Make it perfect Ella. You got this!"

Every day I observed myself in the mirror.

"Do I look more ripped? Did I gain any fat?"

I dieted hard with a typical bodybuilder approach: tilapia, asparagus, chicken, broccoli, and the occasional carb of brown rice and oatmeal for the show. Sometimes, I had almonds or hardboiled eggs, but not often.

I also forcefully drank at least a gallon of water a day. I still wasn't used to actually eating, so all of this was hard to do for me but even with adding some food back into my life, even though it was plain, my body was still starving and it got to the point where I couldn't even look at a peanut butter jar because I'd open it up and eat the whole damn thing.

I started to beg to my mother to stop making brownies, bringing home peanut butter, and even keeping ice cream in the freezer. If it was in the house, I'd find it and eat it all in one sitting. I'd lose my abs, get fat, and hate myself so much that I'd have to go puke it all up.

I was derailing my own progress but continued to blame my surroundings because it was everyone else's fault as to why I was binging, not my own.

It was almost like it was a game to me, that food was weakness. It would make me lose points and the longer I could go without it, the better I would be and the smaller I would become. This was my goal: "Get lean, be lean."

Remember, I'm an extremist at heart, I don't do things halfway, it's all or nothing. So I went hard. I continued to starve myself and train myself into the ground because I wanted it so badly, it was in my heart that I was going to win.

Training Plan during my time in college:	
Mondays	07:00 – 08:30: Weights. 17:00 – 20:00: Classes. 21:00 – 22:00: Cardio.
Tuesdays	05:00 – 06:30: Weights. 08:00 – 16:00: Classes. 17:00 – 18:00: Cardio.
Wednesdays	07:00 – 08:30: Weights. 17:00 – 20:00: Classes. 21:00 – 22:00: Cardio.
Thursdays	05:00 – 06:30: Weights. 08:00 – 16:00: Classes. 17:00 – 18:00: Cardio.
Fridays	07:00 – 08:00: Cardio 17:00 – 18:30: Weights and cardio.
Saturdays	09:00 – 11:30: Weights and cardio.
Sundays	08:00 – 09:00: Cardio 14:00 – 15:00: Weights

Some days would pass by where I only drank black coffee, ate some egg whites in the morning and four ounces of tilapia in the evening. I needed protein and it was about the leanest, shittiest type of protein I could get besides my egg whites.

Oh and by the way, I hate tilapia, it's disgusting, I cannot even eat it to this day unless it's covered in some sort of fancy sauce or crusted with some kind of deliciousness, but I will not touch tilapia by itself, it haunts me.

The kitchen in my household also haunts me. It's where my habits took place, where the demons got their courage to rage, and it just disgusts me greatly because of the power it once had on me. It lurks with all these tainted memories and it has everything that can destroy me within reach.

My very own kitchen is a dark place for me. How sad is that? Yeah, sad. But think about it, you cannot go into your old classrooms and not remember slaving through homework, laughing with your friends, and taking test after test, just as I cannot walk into my very own kitchen and remember slaving through food, crying by myself, and puking binge after binge. I'm saddened by its memories.

I had a terribly hard time dieting that strictly and to not practice any serious binging, but somehow managed to wean away a little bit from it just for a short moment's notice.

The day, in April 2012, that I stepped on stage, I was about 120 pounds and terribly malnourished. My body looked and felt like shit but I went ahead and went through with the show. My muscles were flat, I was shaking out of control, I had a pulsing headache and I really didn't know how to eat, I feared eating. I wanted to eat, but I had to be ripped for the show and if I ate, everything would disappear.

It's in my head that food is the enemy. In reality, nutrition is the biggest factor to whether or not you grow, keep, and have muscle.

The show came and went. I didn't even care to know what I placed, I was almost embarrassed about my physique but I moved on, acting like everything was alright. I was proud, regardless of the outcome, and even with my final package. I did something weird for me, I flexed semi-naked in front of an entire crowd so that a select few could judge me.

What kind of eating disorder person was I? Being basically naked on a stage for all to see, that's bizarre as hell, but back then I believed that I didn't have a problem.

That night I went out to eat with my parents. I inhaled peanut butter cream cakes, brownies with Reese's and peanut butter baked inside them, a cheeseburger loaded with guacamole and bacon, sweet potato french fries smothered in ketchup, giant hot cookies with plenty of scoops of ice cream, root beer and not that diet shit, the real cane sugar kind, and more and more cake. I just couldn't stop eating all this rich food. I felt as if I'd never get the chance again. But really, I was just trying to mask over the sadness inside me; attempting to fill up the emptiness that was swallowing me. It also felt like an easy justification for my binging.

I was trying so hard to numb myself out from the world when really I was just trying to numb out the world from myself.

After exploding into the plethora of comfort food provided to me, I went upstairs to my forbidden escape. I was extremely bloated, the veins in my arms were surging with sugar. The smell of my tan was starting to get to me and so I sat down with a towel in my lap, it was time to puke up all this food. I could only get rid of about half of my damages, it was just so much food that I couldn't throw up anymore due to the exhaustion from my weeks of depletion and the emotional stress of being judged.

That night I cried. My heavy black mascara ran down my face taking away my orange tan with it, my hands cradled my thin face, the fake nails slightly digging into my skin.

I'm saddened greatly by the fact that I had none of my friends there to support me. I really didn't have any friends. People only approached me in those days because I had this following to my name, I was just "that real fit girl". "Go ask her for advice."

'You can change this Ella, you've got to change this.'

But I didn't. I'm not even sure if I tried sometimes, I just let it have me. I just continued to fall on my face day after day.

I constantly binged and purged after the show which caused my tiny body to blow up. I continued to train and strive for greatness. I was still in denial that I had an issue.

A month after my show, in May 2012, I ran the Spartan Sprint in Burnet, Texas, where I came in second place.

Shrug. I had hardly been running, my body was out of shape due to the excessive eating, and my hormones were just about nonexistent. So I found some acceptance with placing so 'low'. Anything less than first place back then to me just wasn't good enough. I was tired of being the underdog in life. But that's what I did, I rose and I fell, I am the ultimate underdog, or cheetah we can say.

Enjoy my recollection.

I struggled with anorexia and bulimia off and on during 2011 to 2012 but it didn't seem to really take a hold of me too much. Or maybe I was just in too much denial about it.

Then, in early 2013, I shattered my foot in two places. This caused me to not be able to run, not be able to properly train. I became lost in my complicated disorder and I could see no way out of it. I was at rock bottom and fuck man, it just really sucked.

I couldn't seem to be able to starve myself anymore so I ditched anorexia, the whole not eating thing became severely dull for me and so I started to go overboard with food. Oh yeah, bulimia became my new beloved monster from there on out.

It was inevitable for me though, I couldn't go on starving myself much longer without finding myself getting hospitalized due to heart failure.

I want to be something great.

I want to be something great.

I want to be something great.

So at the end of 2012 and the beginning of 2013 my playground, the one which I had once run around so happily in, was now destroyed by my very own hands.

I was that poor craftsman who used tools that were too cheap to create his masterpiece and watched helplessly as his creation crumbled in front of his very own eyes.

Shit dude, I wish there was a more significant moment, that was filled with trauma, that took me to the next stage in my life. 2013 was, without a doubt, the darkest I have been and was my roughest year yet. Now, while I write this only a year after its incidents, I am happy to expose it for I am in a much better place.

I am just so obsessed with being great.

We all have our highs and our lows, here is my lowest of my lows thus far. Welcome to my 2013. Welcome to my char-boiled heart, seasoned with confusion and dipped in a depressing sauce of hatred for life.

Get your forks ready, it's time to destroy your sanity.

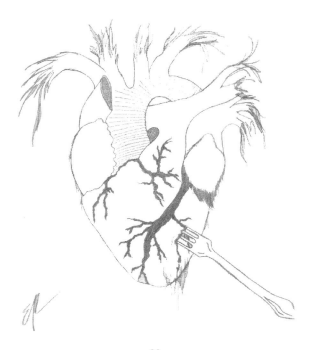

Give me mud. Give me scars.

Do you want to know what it's like inside the head of someone who battles with an eating disorder? Parallel lines, not even once.

The burning in the eyes. I won't do it again.

The raging cramps inside my guts. This is the last time, I swear.

The pulse in the back of my throat. I won't do this again.

The feeling of scraping my throat open. This is the last time, I swear.

The numbness in my fingers. I won't do this again.

The stomach acid sizzling in my gums. This is the last time, I swear.

The immediate feel of self-hate. I know better.

The immediate feel of guilt. Why this again?

The immediate feel of confusion. I know better.

The immediate feel of stupidity. Why this again?

The immediate feel of loneliness. I know better.

The immediate feel of lack of control. Why this again?

The immediate feel of darkness. I know better.

I purposely made sure to make the feeling of darkness and the statement in my head, 'I know better' be last on the list because it was the scariest, it was also the hardest to understand, the hardest to get over, the hardest to deny, the hardest to fake, the hardest to forget, and the hardest to let go of.

It controls you.

The simple fact of knowing better and being lost in the darkness is a dirty habit.

The pain felt like an addiction and it controlled all of me.

I couldn't stop cycling it.

I was unaware of my buyer's actual face.

It ruined my family time.

It ruined my social time.

It ruined my money.

It ruined my health.

It ruined me.

FUCK FORKS.

I felt bad but I still took its poison.

I had an addiction and I really wanted to let it go.

I had a disorder and I really wanted it to let me go.

I had a demon inside me and I really wanted it to let me be.

I had an emptiness inside me and I really wanted it to fill it.

I'm a fighter. That's what I've learned to do.

I'm a struggler. That's what I've learned to endure.

I'm a believer. That's what I've learned to be.

"I'll just have a bite. That looks so good."

"But Ella, one little bite that's off your nutrition guidelines and you'll binge. It happens every time and you know it."

"No, no, not this time, it'll be different."

"I just want food."

"Just a bite."

"I need to eat."

"What the hell?"

"Fuck, I'm such a pig."

"Oh well, I already messed up, might as well just destroy myself."

"I can't even taste this."

"But this is so good."

"Hurry, before Dad comes home."

"What was that noise?"

"Hide the food."

"Stuff your face faster, faster."

"The day's already ruined."

"I'm ruined."

"Ah, it's okay why not."

"Just do it already."

"You know you want to."

"Look at yourself, stop it."

"No, no. I need this."

"I need it."

"I need it."

"Shut up."

After a few hard days of over eating and less purging, the damage was starting to really show physically, so much that I didn't even see my own reflection anymore.

"There is nothing looking back at me" I said. "This is not me, this is not me. THIS IS NOT ME." But is it?

Who is Ella Anne Kociuba?

There was a demon inside me I could not seem to get a grip of.

I lost control.

There was a demon inside me who I could not seem to understand.

I lost reasoning.

There was a demon inside me that I feared so much.

I lost faith.

There was a demon inside me and when he came out...

I lost myself.

Sometimes I wanted to dig my head so deep into the ground that I could not breathe, so deep that even the roots that caved into the darkness began to beg for light. I wanted my sorrows to swallow me. I was ready for a breakdown.

Let it come, I want it.

It was so disgusting how much I wanted to be weak in those very moments that not even the strongest alcoholic drink could make sense of it. The pulse in my chest drove my mind insane, and I did not know how to grasp this. But at the same time it was all way too familiar and I could predict my fate.

The fact that I know this, causes an uncontrollable ache of frustration.

I know better, I know what's going to come of this.

Oh, that's disgusting.

The burning sensation in my eyes began to grow and before I knew it, hot, heavy droplets of tears streamed down my face, covering my cheeks with their evidence of pain. I cannot deny my strain.

"Why, oh why am I here?"

My body began to sway in motion, pacing my negativity back and forth as if I could shake it off. But even I knew that that was just silly. This was my breakdown and I had welcomed it by giving up.

This was my moment of weakness and it was swallowing me whole.

Every binge was just like the other, it generally started with an empty feeling inside my gut even if I had just consumed an entire meal. I oddly felt as if something was missing and without thinking too much about it, I would be standing on a chair, sifting through the back of the cabinets, grabbing chips or cookies. Then I'd walk over to the fridge, pull the cheese drawer open and stuff the slices in my mouth. I'd be walking over to the bread box, pulling out tortillas, bread, English muffins and layering them with cheese or peanut butter. Throw them in the microwave, heat them up, stuff them in my face. Next, I'd walk back over to the cabinets, get out a different kind of peanut butter, smear it on some cookies, eat that too, crumble the other cookies onto some bread, heat that up too, dip it into some honey. Sugar rush. On to the search for meat because the sugar was giving me a headache which was always followed by severe stomach cramps. I know all of this real well. So I stuffed deli meat into my mouth, stuffed the cheese sticks down my throat, chugged some cranberry juice. I'd pause for a moment, out of breath, and look down at my bloated stomach.

"Alright, it's time to get rid of all this."

I grabbed a long fork from the drawers, went upstairs, sat down in front of my toilet, stuck my fingers down until they didn't work anymore, then put the long fork down my throat.

I really hate forks.

I forcefully puked until I saw blood. Sometimes I'd puke so hard that I'd piss my pants but that didn't faze me whatsoever, I could change my pants once I was done destroying myself.

After puking for what felt like a light year, I'd then go look at my red eyes and check out my stomach in the mirror.

"Where's my abs?"

"What am I doing to myself?"

Not long after, I'd be back downstairs where I was back to eating everything in sight.

Repeat, repeat, repeat, this was my life.

During most binges I often ate without actually ever tasting the food and if there wasn't anything really to binge on, I'd go back and forth from spooning out jars of peanut butter and ice cream to chomping down cheese. These things we always seemed to have.

You soon get smart enough to figure out what's easy to throw up and which foods hurt more. Purging is an act, almost an art form at that. You can either be real good at it or real sucky, but either way it's going to hurt, so you might as well make it slightly enjoyable.

My go-to foods for easy puking were: yogurt, oatmeal, cottage cheese, peanut butter, ice cream, applesauce, cool whip, and if I was lucky, there would be my mother's left over brownies. If you heat them up just right, it's like this hot chocolate bread of sex in your mouth that dissolves as soon as it hits your anxious tongue.

But I didn't always pick foods that were delicious, simply because we didn't always have them around, so I would eat whatever there was in the house. Sometimes I would binge on water crackers, bitter sweet chocolate chips, saltines with cream cheese, potato chips, dried fruit, almonds, salted cashews, 100 calorie sliced thin bread with jelly, whip cream, bananas smothered in honey, just anything that was handy and didn't require any real wait time or work.

During some of my purging, I would bring my laptop into the bathroom, put on some sad music and read fan mail.

"Ella, you've inspired me, I want to thank you…"

It all broke my heart, I didn't feel worthy of any of it.

I really don't know why I used to read my emails in between making myself vomit. Maybe I was trying to find something that would help me to turn this around, that would make me stop and realize that I had people who care for me, but it was like an addiction. I couldn't just stop it cold turkey even when I read things like "you saved my life", I'd chuckle in a sick manner. "Can you save mine, please?"

I sat there with stomach acid all over my mouth, a towel filled with throw up and blood that didn't make it to the toilet, a fork in my left hand shaking from all the emotions, heavy tears dripping off my chin, and only the sound of emptiness that resides inside my heart filling the space around me.

"I am not worthy of your praise. You have no idea how sick I am."

I cried and cried and oh man did I cry. I did not trip and fall onto my knees. No, oh hell no, I fell straight onto my face, every damn time, over and over again.

Back then, I used to pity my own self. I repeatedly told myself that no one should ever envy me, no one should look up to me because look at this, I'm pathetically lost in this mess and I can't seem to get my shit together. I bashed myself into the ground for my flaws.

I couldn't seem to see that having these flaws were actually showing me just how strong I truly was in a very unique way.

My flaws are just like a cheetah's spots. They all have their own unique shape but they fit me, they are forever a part of me even if they are placed a little differently than the rest.

These flaws are just my cheetah spots, but I didn't see them in this light yet to appreciate them.

On a brighter note, I sure did create some really awesome food inventions during my binging. Like stuffing white chocolate macadamia nut Cliff Bars into a peanut butter and jelly sandwich that's also stuffed with chocolate chips, real berries, almonds, and Oreos!

Oh yeah, I would go all out, it's all or nothing for me baby.

My binging was really dangerous. Well, any type of binging is, but I took it to an extreme level of stupidity. I would make sure that every time I purged, I would keep going until I saw some blood come up, until all I had left was acid and my torn insides to gag up. That way I would know I had gotten all the food out of my system, that I was 'clean'.

How could I ever want this? How could I ever put this upon myself? It may have been a minor slip up or a huge fall, but nonetheless, the pain haunted me.

I was living in a constant feeling of shame and guilt. Everything, no matter how simple it was, became complicated and I ended up becoming a constant hesitation and a constant flake. I didn't want to see anyone nor did I want anyone to see me. I didn't even know who 'me' was. Maybe I liked that part about it, that I controlled myself so abusively that I was able to develop a tragic fairy tale that would end in me becoming something great.

Besides, life is painful sometimes you know.

I'm in a love hate relationship with pain, it's my life long partner.

The moment that toppled me over and caused me to crack underneath my demons' demands, both physically and mentally, happened shortly after I began my season of obstacle and adventure racing in spring of 2013.

April 29th, 2013:

I felt silly, but at the same time I could not hold back the tears. They were inevitable at that moment. I bit my lip in attempts to suppress the pain as my mind raced through the situation, I was sidelined yet again.

I traced my mind back to the moment I remembered the pain in my foot and began to beat myself up.

Why didn't I stop then?

Why didn't I go to a doctor sooner?

Why did this happen to me?

Why did I run in that race?

Why now?

WHY?

WHY?

WHY?

Why, oh why am I here?

Give me mud. Give me scars.

Then as quickly as my negativity soaked into me, I shook my head and told myself that this could be much worse. I'm being a little bitch. AND THIS LITTLE BITCH WANTS TO EAT!

But at the same time, all I could really think about was the past and also how messed up my future seemed now. Everything turned grey. There was no more color in my vision and I was overwhelmed by a deep sadness that cuddled up into my chest, causing me to struggle while swallowing.

Not this again. Get away.

My doctor explained to me that I had a longitudinal tear in my right foot. I had torn the brevis and longus tendons.

Splendid.

Later that I day, I found myself moaning around. Digging my frustration out of a gallon of Blue Bell's vanilla ice cream and it was just plain vanilla, I don't even care for plain vanilla ice cream. It was all we had at home and so it was going down. I then went to a Sonic later that day to get a Reese's cup blast to eat in my truck all by myself. I sat there crying with no intentions of fighting the emotions, I just let them come.

WANT TO GO AWAY NOW!

I couldn't tell why exactly I was crying so hard at that moment. The injury was nothing compared to everything else I had faced but I was just downright tired of it all. I was tired of the war I am in with my body and I couldn't seem to find the peace I wanted.

I was always hurt, but you couldn't even see the majority of my pain because it lived inside my head and heart.

Guilt and sorrow.

Can I have your leg to borrow?

Give me mud. Give me scars.

I turned twenty on June 21, 2013. To those who did not know me, and even those who did, I appeared to be the happiest girl on the planet. My smile was huge, my attitude still holding onto its edge, and my eyes glowing with life.

But I was a good liar, or at least I tried to be.

I fooled my family, my friends, my fans, and my sponsors into believing I was healthy all of this time. Occasionally I would drop hints of my hurt, but never was able to fully admit it or say "help, I have a problem". So I hid the darkness inside me. Unfortunately, it weighed so heavily on my mind that it caused me to become distant from not only those around me but from myself and I got lost in the dark. The familiarity of wandering amongst its empty streets, its filthy walls, and its cold temperatures was scarily comfortable. This controlling habit wasn't just a phase, it was a lifestyle for me and it was all I knew how to do right.

That summer, I began to eat even more than I ever had before and boy did I eat a lot. I went on extreme binges of anywhere from 1,000 to 3,000 calories per sitting, at least five times a day.

At first I used my fingers then my long forks to purge it up, but within time they began to not do their job and so I was then forced to use only a long fork.

I was sucked into a vicious cycle and I couldn't seem to help myself. Gradually my five times a day began to be twenty times a day.

I was the definition of a successful tragedy but no one really knew that about me yet.

Enjoy my heartache.

The darkness that I wandered around in started way before that moment in time. So let's go back to 2011, to when I was eighteen and saw the world as my playground.

I had all the tools in my hands to create something great but my obsessive characteristics caused me to build off of irrational emotions and so I created my empire with unreliable sources, only to have it all quickly crumble beneath me.

I want to be something great.

I want to be something great.

I want to be something great.

I was told by someone, who is to remain nameless, to eat about eight hundred calories a day with little-to-no carbs while I was running anywhere from fifty-five to seventy miles a week and lifting weights six to seven times a week.

This was the start of my explosive downfall. I am the Triple Crown winner, chomping at its bit, swallowing its own blood (literally). Where is my fame?

Bite your lip; swallow.

I told myself that this was digging deep, this was the way champions were made; they make sacrifices. This was how it was supposed to be. But little did I know, I was very far from the truth and even farther from ever being truly victorious.

Throughout my early days of training, I basically starved myself and began to pass out on the benches outside my classrooms or in the computer room in between classes at the local community college I was attending at the time.

As previously stated, I was still making sure that for every calorie I ate, I would burn the same amount off at the gym or even better, burn more. I was so obsessed with calories that I would praise the days I ate 500 or less.

When it came to race day, I would somehow manage to come toppling out at first place female in just about every single event I entered into and it dumbfounded me.

Why, oh why am I here?

My severe body aches become a normality. Going to bed at eight o'clock every night only to awake at five was my way of life. I told myself over and over that I enjoyed this.

I got this.

I also developed sports related amenorrhoea, a condition that females can get from having too little body fat combined with the hormones released during physical exercise, which can cause an absence in menstruation cycles. But I never sought out any medical help due to the simple fact that I believed that it was the way it had to be.

And besides, I got this. I'M STRONG!

I was also quite embarrassed about the issues popping up so I resorted to ignoring any medical issue I found and put it into a small place inside my head, putting the dead cat underneath the rug, they didn't exist if I didn't acknowledge them.

I GOT THIS.

Every race ritual went as the follows:

A couple of days prior to the race I would have a small binge due to anxiety, then manage any weight gain by doing the stair-master for at least an hour or more.

The night before the race I'd make sure to puke everything up, even though it was hardly anything.

BE AS LIGHT AS POSSIBLE.

My sleep habits suffered from the pain in my stomach, my throat, and my mind, so I only got about three to four hours of sleep.

In the morning I would awaken to bloodshot eyes from the damaging efforts and exertion of my forceful puking. I went as far as getting eye drops to help calm them, to cover everything up. I'd brush my teeth to make sure the smell of acid and vomit was not lingering on me but sometimes I would get a whiff of it even after spraying myself down, it was always a part of me.

Three hours before my event, I would actually make sure to eat a meal which usually consisted of a bowl of oatmeal with banana, some honey, and protein powder. But most of the times I could hardly finish the bowl.

I really do not know how I even competed so well back then, but I did. I would either win or come in the top three and regardless of what type of competition it was, I was guaranteed a new personal record at just about every event I attended.

This sick way to success I had created had brainwashed me.

My family would celebrate my victories by taking me out to fancy restaurants where I would finally get the taste of what food was like in my mouth.

I'd chomp down so hard onto my bit in these moments when I anticipated my fall prematurely and I'd weaken down underneath my demons' demands. This flavorful surge of emotions pushed me into stuffing all types of food into my mouth. Anything and everything I saw I would eat, or should I say inhale.

Immediately after the hype of my binge slows, I was absorbed by the feeling of guilt from eating actual food, and from the insane Santa Clause stomach I now had, so I begin to casually puke up my meals.

The days after the race would go like this: binge and puke, binge and puke, then finally I'd get back on my 'grind' of little to no food and to training like a mad woman.

As odd as it sounds, it was almost comfortable for me to be like this, it was way too easy to be extreme. The control of food became an intriguing action for me to perform, even though I hated the way purging made me feel. I would be covered in tears, snot, and vomit while lost in the pathetic attempts to dry out my stomach with my little body lunged over the toilet seat hurling out acid.

Life was painful and I really didn't get why I was there.

This became my ritual and I could not seem to compete without it.

Bulimia got an even more selfish grip on my life and took a hold of the few normal eating habits I had left.

YOU DON'T DESERVE TO FEEL GOOD.

It became so evil that even if I did not binge on food, I would make sure to purge it up immediately. Shit, it didn't even matter if I was going to compete in a grueling event the next day, I would feel guilty about just eating and inside my head I had to get it out of me.

It was black and white, all or nothing, this is what I must do.

A typical day for me began with the thoughts:

"New day"

"No binging today"

"Turn it around"

"Remember how terrible you felt yesterday?"

"Don't fuck up"

"You got this"

But all my self-talk would turn to shit immediately after eating my breakfast which consisted of egg whites with spinach and oatmeal with peanut butter.

YOU'RE SO PATHETIC.

Something within me surged and the voices in my head took over me. I went numb, I wandered around the kitchen from fridge to pantry, to the freezer, to the fridge again, to the cabinets, and then over to my special peanut butter cabinet. I mixed foods, I recreated more oatmeal with chocolate chips, peanut butter, cool whip, I then I'd go get the tortillas and stuff them with left over salmon, cheese, and chug some chocolate milk because it was looking at me.

Nachos, I should make nachos, I get chips and a plate, dump cheese all over it and heat it up, as the microwave zaps my food with its rays, I go back to the cabinet and find the Biscoff cookies, eat them with more peanut butter as my other hand continues to search the back of the cabinet. The timer goes off and I hurried over to the microwave and began to eat the nachos rapidly, not even tasting them.

I'M SO FAT, I'LL NEVER BE GREAT.

Oh man, ice cream, I needed ice cream now. I searched through the freezer and what would I find? Oh goody, mother's old apple cake, I'd pull it out and get the vanilla beam ice cream. I couldn't even wait to heat up the cake so I begin to stab it with my fork, fuck forks! I stuffed my face with its sugary endorphins.

Numb me. Cure me.

Not only was I addicted to my self-image but I was addicted to, and longed for, pain. I loved it, I lived it, I was it. At the same time, I avoided it and searched for comfort. What's better than comfort food? What's better than making yourself throw up until you bleed for pain? Yes, my mind was that fucked up.

I was lost in this belief that I was doing the right thing even if it felt extremely sadistic and wrong at times. But perhaps, I was just that way.

I could feel how ruined my mind was becoming and even my own body. But that was not important because I was still winning titles, so I ignored it.

Not long after working so hard through my achy life, the strive to become something great started to become an unimpressive goal and I found that it even felt overrated to hold up a trophy, to smile for the cameras, and show off my hard work with selfies or tight clothing.

I started to really hate social media and all the eyes around me. I felt so unworthy of everything but I ignored that feeling too, I ignored that I was tired of trying so hard and remained lost in this notion of finding 'success' and being 'great' through my self-harm.

It was engrained inside my mind that my bulimia wasn't an issue, it was just a way of life for me. My binging and purging would get me to perfection one day and I believed that I was actually in control of this.

When I think about it now, a couple of years later, I realize that, in a way, bulimia completed me. I enjoyed the fact that I was out of control but in control of that. While I was growing up the only thing that ever had control of me was pain, so this infliction of pain and 'controlling' seemed fitting for me.

At the time it also seemed to be the only option for me and somehow my season of racing went surprisingly well even though I was constantly sick.

I slept between training sessions, all while consuming just enough calories to be able to read my biology reports or type up my short stories for English class.

Acquaintances asked me to hangout, asked me for nutrition and training advice, I gave them advice, I told them to eat food, to sleep well, take care of themselves, love themselves, be happy, and train hard. I told them everything I needed to be told.

As I gave advice to so many others, I was really just trying to talk to myself but I couldn't seem to listen. I was actually the one who really needed someone to help me but I couldn't admit that yet.

If you didn't already assume, you're right on the fact that, yes I still had no social life. My best friend had left my side long ago due to my strive for greatness in the fitness world, and the few individuals I met at college didn't seem to hold my attention. The people around me spoke of parties, drugs, and drinking while all I could think of was training, food, and competing. This left me very alone in my own little sick world. I was a young adolescent in college and I hated the thought of drinking or doing any type of drug. My addiction was this disorder, it was also my body and my performance that I'd never let go of.

Social life was nonexistent as I started to obsess more about my food. I wanted complete control of everything that entered my belly. But really it was food that controlled me, and sure enough, I feared going out to eat. I didn't like it when others cooked for me. If I ever did go out to eat, I'd ask:

"Did you put oil on this?"

"How do you prepare your chicken?"

"Is there butter on your vegetables?"

I needed to know these things, and if I didn't know, I began to feel my heart race, the walls started to tilt, my feet started tapping the ground like there was an imaginary brake pedal in this truck that was headed towards a cliff.

I'm going to die.

MAKE IT STOP.

My behavior weakened underneath its constant screaming and I started to quiver inside just at the thought of hanging out with friends. I couldn't stand the stress that social gatherings brought me because I simply just didn't trust myself. What was even sicker about that situation was that the few friends I had from the gym shared this exact feeling, so I got the false pretense that this was still right. My surroundings told me that complete restriction was how you get to be successful.

Roger that.

LIE TO ME MORE ELLA.

I am a big social unicorn. I laugh loudly, make inappropriate jokes, break the ice with crazy hugs, and just simply love to meet people.

So I did try to go out and be social, but if there was queso and chips at the party, I'd eat the entire thing and it wouldn't stop there. I'd leave that party, go home and raid the cabinets, stuff my face with all kinds of food, grab a long fork, go to the toilet upstairs, forcefully put it past my tongue, puke it all back up, go cry in my bed for a little bit, then go cry back in my bathroom while I stared at myself.

"Look how pathetic you are."

I'd then walk back downstairs after chugging some water, open the fridge and stare at it. Did something new appear? No, but I would always find something to stuff to my face with. I inhaled more calories than I could withstand, walked around in circles with my hands touching my face.

I always touch my face when I'm nervous, anxious, and confused.

HIDE MY FACE.

I really didn't want to find myself submerged into that chaos, so it was easy for me to just isolate myself, to avoid possible situations, and to distract my mind from what seemed to be the inevitable. So I became a lone wolf.

Going out to eat or going out with friends made me incredibly anxious and I could not bear the thought of doing it, so I flaked from party invites, dinners, get togethers, and lunches because I didn't trust myself.

I wanted to be alone, it was easy.

Even if I had wanted to talk to someone about the heaviness in my head, I didn't have anyone to really relate to. The few friends that I did have at the time had no idea of my struggles and only saw me as the 'fitness goddess', which is such a silly thought now. While sure, my outside appearances back then may have looked aesthetically pleasing in some aspects, my insides were failing me.

Yes, this pathetic image was me. It was what I did and I did it for two years quietly until my injuries from my disorder got out of control and the evidence of my habits started to show.

Give me mud. Give me scars.

After my first victory in 2011, I entered myself into every race I could, and I was winning road races and obstacle races left and right. At the same time, my name was growing into something the fitness community recognized.

Before I could even realize it, I had collected a following of supporters and it was the oddest, most bizarre thing to me.

People actually like me?

The buzz of social media threw new opportunities at me and therefore I decided to take on bigger events with the new support of sponsorships.

So I traveled to Pittsfield, Vermont to compete in the Spartan Summer Death Race of 2011. The theme of the race was 'Betrayal'.

I was rather lean a couple weeks prior to the Death Race. Lean enough for my six pack abdominals to show, for my shoulders to be striated, and for the veins in my forearms to be a roadmap. I was aesthetically pleasing to the eye.

But the pressure of this race got to me. The pressure of being great, perfect, and successful dumped me right back into my familiar life of being a bulimic person.

That summer my mother's peach trees grew an insane amount of peaches and so I ate an insane amount of peaches. The week before the race, I stuffed my belly with peaches, peach bread, peach muffins, peach jam and peach pie. I got so big and round that I looked like a damn peach going to the Death Race. None of my clothes would fit me, and I still couldn't stop eating those damn peaches, and whatever else I saw, even leading up to the very last moments before I went out into the mountains to race.

Going into the event, I was very uneducated on what it was like to really grind with a rucksack drilling into your traps and the hurt of what hiking on a mountain aimlessly for days felt like. I also wasn't aware of the mental fuck I was getting myself into and boy did it mess me up something nasty.

My body began to show the evidence of the internal damage through this event.

Thirty three hours in, after carrying a tractor tire up the mountains for about twenty hours with an inspiring group of people I got paired up with, we were known as team 10 (also known as team tire), completing other tasks like chopping wood, running time trials, remembering quotes on betrayal, and lots of other craziness, my body stopped working for me and I ended up limping with severe pain coming from my right leg.

So I ended up DNF'ing (Did Not Finish) due to a hairline fracture in my tibia and it crushed my soul.

The injury itself didn't seem to affect me mentally, but the fact that I had to quit was something that began to tear me up inside slowly throughout the next year.

It was the first event of my life that I failed at and it was the first race that began to change my mindset, to look down at my shoes and really appreciate them.

My post-race ritual of binging and purging commenced like usual but I found myself able to recover from it within two weeks. Still tubby in the midsection, I returned to training and found myself extremely determined to turn my season around.

So I came back from my tibia injury too soon and ended up re-busting open the same shin while running the Pennsylvania Spartan Sprint in July of 2012. In a very dramatic finish, I came out in fifth place and was promptly escorted off on a gator and taken off to the emergency room not far from the race venue.

I get out for another moment's notice and returned back again in the fall to compete in several other Spartan Races, including placing third in the Vermont Beast Championships in September 2012.

I finished the rest of my season off with a shrug. I did all of this while being sick with my bulimia which mainly circled around my races. It took me another year to realize that my world was a very fucked up place in regards to what I lived for, that the thing that made me the happiest also made me the saddest and I was addicted to pain because I was comfortable with it.

I'd never be good enough in my own eyes if I continued to live this way.

Getting exhausted from purging and witnessing my teeth beginning to show evidence of stomach acid, the gears began to turn inside my tainted head and so I thought of other ways to get rid of my food.

When I discovered the beauty of laxatives and thermogenics, I started enforcing them into my twisted world of food control and obsessive training. I drank a diet tea every night, took colon cleanses, took a fat burner morning and night, and even sat inside saunas before and after every workout to help sweat out any water weight.

The laxatives started to corrupt some of my training runs in the mornings but it wasn't a big deal to me. I ran off the trails and popped a squat like the little nature child I am. The food started to go just straight through me and I started starving more than ever. I was a malnourished beast, but as long as my abdominals ware tight and I won my races, I was alright.

The ache of greatness still resided inside my bones and finally I recovered from my tibia injury. With the news of good health, I began my 2013 season in high spirits. I dropped my eating disorder behaviors and got rigid with my mindset. I started eating clean, training hard, sleeping well again.

2013 would be mine.

Clocking in my training runs at 5:42 minute miles, 235 pound back squats, 95 pound bench, and a body frame at 136 pounds, I was on top of my game. I even seemed to believe that I didn't have an eating disorder anymore. I had gone six weeks without any huge binges and declared myself as 'sober'.

However, I was just at that part of the roller coaster where everyone smiles in joy for a brief moment. But we all know there's soon to be a drop and we're going to scream our lungs out.

I'M GOING TO PUKE MINE OUT.

My season started with my first race over in Arizona for the Spartan Sprint, and it was expected to be a showdown between myself and two other athletes.

Nervous as ever, I attended the race with some doubt that I would not place high enough for my likings but still believed that I could manage it.

"Manage it, Ella. Just believe in yourself."

The race ended up being the closest one I had ever ran to date, and throughout the course I switched lead roles with two other athletes.

With each change in leader, I was still so uncertain if I could manage it.

Manage that win.

Manage that pain.

Five seconds stood on the clock between second place and myself that day. It was a victory where even the medal and the money weren't what made me cry in happiness, it was the battle inside myself that caused tears to burst from my face.

I treasured the raw emotions from that day, and after that race I believed that I was back in action, that this was going to be my year. As it turned out, it was my year, my year to break down and face death. It wasn't the year of my rising like I had hoped for.

After the Arizona race, I came home and binged for two days but quickly turned it around. I hit training even harder. I was still semi clean from my eating disorder, and I was crushing life's demands.

Not long after Arizona I travelled up to North Carolina to compete in another Spartan Sprint. The temperatures that day ranged anywhere from 28 to 36 degrees with rain that fell sideways during the whole event. It was easily one of the fastest times I had run, despite slipping off of a lot of simple obstacles due to the ice and mud. I came out in first place again, screaming my head off.

My second race of the season and my second win, it was my comeback.

"Look at me everyone!"

Whether I realized it or not, eyes were watching my every move and I got so caught up in the feeling of being invincible that I ignored my internal issues even more than ever.

I made the common mistake of overtraining and returned back to the trails as soon as I settled into my home in Texas. I went out for some mile repeats on the trails with my mind already locked down onto my next event which was only two weeks away; the Spartan Super in Las Vegas.

The race had attracted some of the biggest named athletes in my league and the money prize for it went up to $5,000 for first place. Everyone wanted a taste of that victory.

I seemed to be able taste it already from my time on top so far and it was a bittersweet sensation to my taste buds. Its sweetness, however, seemed to be too weak for my tasting and I desperately searched for more of it to fill my appetite. Perhaps I was too much of a bottomless pit to find satisfaction with my first few bites and just like the fine sugar upon my lips, my bones became just as innocent as its molecules and I crumbled.

Something sharp went off in the side of my foot on my third mile and I crumbled down to the ground.

This tasted really damn bitter.

I needed something much sweeter than this now. Licking my lips, the sweetness had faded and I realized my time at the top and my precious chance at another victory died immediately with a simple crack in my foot.

Pour some sugar on me baby, I'm bitter.

The pain in my foot disabled my running abilities, so I laid off of it. The aches ate at me leading up to the race but I decided to not let it stop me and attended the event anyways.

The race was about eight miles long with elevation changes that caused you to break into a hike instead of a run while the dry desert heat burned into your skin.

This race crushed my ego as I suffered through it and came out in a very close fourth place. With the pain in my foot radiating as I limped across the finish line, the words "I probably shouldn't have done that" settled into my head. And it became quite clear that whatever was up with my foot was something serious and that I was seriously stupid.

When I returned back home a few days after spending some time fattening myself up at buffets in Vegas with my father, I went to my foot doctor who informed me of my ruptured tendons. My tendons weren't the only thing ruptured at this moment, my heart seemed to have ruptured with the news and I watched helplessly as my time at the top was terminated instantly.

Goodbye greatness.

I went through phases of pure negativity then acceptance of the situation while telling myself "This too shall pass and I will return back to competing in no time, this injury is nothing compared to my past."

However, my foot did not seem to want to heal and I was left with an uncertainty as to when I would be able to return back to competing. So I began to sulk down into a depressive state about my pitiful little struggle and I wound up getting swallowed by the demon inside me... AGAIN.

At that point in time I was on a high fat diet where my carbohydrates were less than 30 grams, my fats were around 160 grams and my protein count was up to 200 grams.

After collapsing hard from this diet and not being able to maintain it, I tried the ketogenic diet, which was almost exactly like my previous diet. My intake slightly changes to a carbohydrate consumption of less than 25 grams a day, fats were up to about 200 grams, and my protein intake was somewhere around 130 grams.

The lack of carbohydrates drove me insane as I ramped up my training and it ended up making me binge even harder and feel crazier, especially when going through ketosis.

I was licking my Tupperwares clean of the olive oil that was on my plain chicken, eating almonds and steamed broccoli like they were potato chips, and stuffing pulled pork in my face.

The diet drove me too feel even hungrier than when I was starving myself. Sure enough, I failed at these diets and ended up falling back to resorting to my oh-so-wonderful cycle of binging, purging, and being down-right depressed. But in a way, it was comfortable for me due to its familiar feeling.

I was back at the cabinets, the fridge and the freezer, walking around stuffing my face with dry cereal, licking spoons full of peanut butter, heating up cheese and tortillas, sifting through the back of the pantry to find my mother's hidden chocolates. I ate so many flavorful things without even tasting their flavors in attempts to ignore my hurt.

FALLING ON MY FACE.

My favorite pair of jeans didn't fit my butt anymore, my spandex shorts were too tight around my waist, making me have a muffin top, my once lean hamstrings now showed cellulite, the vascularity in my arms was gone, and my once comfortable sports bra was now tight as hell around my chest.

I was molding into this soft sadness and the worst part about it was that I was doing all this to myself and I couldn't seem to stop it.

So I became lost in my eating disorder again and it almost felt right. I returned back to my old ways, the ways of becoming numb and stuffing my face with food as a coping method to deal with life. But no matter what I ate, I was still truly miserable inside myself. I was unable to train properly and I was putting on the pounds with each passing day.

My obsession was killing me.

Constantly strangers approached me and asked when I would compete again or what was going on with me as of right then. I didn't know the answers to these questions.

I tried to avoid the eyes but they seemed to be everywhere for me, at the gym, the gas station, the grocery store, at the bank, and even in the doctor's office, the eyes were there to watch me.

I CANNOT ESCAPE THE EYES.

I feared that they could see how fat I had become and it was painfully embarrassing for me. They just didn't know what I was dealing with.

Judge me, judge me, judge me please.

Watch me fall.

Watch me rise.

Watch me fail.

Watch me win.

I went back and forth, rising and falling throughout the summer as I attended physical therapy once a week for the following three months.

Even with the progress I made with my injury, it didn't seem to ease me much due to the loss of my sanity from what had already occurred to me. I didn't know what normality was or even what peace felt like between the mind and the body. Therefore, bulimia became a constant ritual in my daily life and it got so bad that I found myself suffering through the cycles at least twenty times a day.

PUKE UNTIL THERE'S BLOOD.

I was smart enough to stop the purging after a while, day by day the purging decreased but the weight began to seriously pack on with each extensive binge I performed.

I started lying to my friends as to why I couldn't go out. I skipped some workouts, hid behind hoodies and sweats, and at night I laid awake with a gut that just might explode with a simple poke. My tender eyes were swollen from tears of confusion and searched the ceiling for answers.

Why, oh why am I here?

I easily went from a 136 pound, 12 percent body fat frame to a 166 pound, 30 percent body fat frame by the end of the summer. Due to my hatred of scales I never weighted myself but if I were to guess, these were my final numbers.

I put on at least thirty, sloppy pounds that collected everywhere and I hated to go anywhere in public.

WHO AM I ANYMORE?

At this point in my life I had completely isolated myself from friends, family, my sponsors, and competitions. I was quiet in the shadows of my own mistakes and it seemed that I had been forgotten by the eyes that once looked at me so eagerly. Hell, I kind of liked it. The simplicity in being so fucking alone in my own misery was like a full time job. My self-abuse and hatred took away my time, my life, my mind, my body, my family, my friends, my everything. I was dedicated to destroying myself.

Towards the end of the summer of 2013, I was requested to make some appearances in the public eye for a few of my sponsors at fit expos and also to go on some tours.

I was still binging on a daily basis and still unable to train well. I collapsed into the cycle of shame with my body. Even though I was embarrassed to do so, oddly enough I found that pretending like everything was okay came quite naturally to me. I attempted to cover up the hurt inside my mind, pretend that I hadn't gained an insane amount of weight for my body frame, and that I didn't have any internal issues going on. The only thing wrong with me was the injury to my foot and that will soon be long gone, I was mending.

Alright, just leave me be.

I told myself these things, these lies which declared that I was okay, I was going to be okay, I was okay!

HAHA, THAT'S SUCH A BIG LIE AND YOU KNOW IT.

I was so absorbed by the lies that I told myself repetitively that finally my personality took a hit for the worst and I lost my giggles. I couldn't even seem to talk anymore. Plus, my smiles that everyone knew me by were nowhere to be found. There was no light in my misery. I was eaten whole by the sorrow that I felt and not once did I acknowledge the change within myself until it was too late.

I hid my binging from my parents and friends, I made sure that my habits went unseen from outsiders as I went through my routine of having no thought process and having just the action of food to mouth.

A few times, my parents would walk in and see me standing there in front of the fridge holding the tub of leftovers or next to the cabinet with my hands in the cereal box. Occasionally they'd ask what I was doing and I would respond with "I haven't eaten all day" or "I'm starving".

I went as far as standing with a pint of ice cream behind my back waiting for them to leave my sights so I could run upstairs and eat my life away.

I needed it, I hated it, I loved it, I lived it. IT WAS MINE.

I didn't answer calls because at any given moment I might break into a loud cry. I didn't go out to enjoy the sun because, in my mind, my body was disgusting. I didn't even want to look at myself. I didn't go on any dates or see anyone because I hated to be touched or looked at. I refused to look into mirrors, step on scales, or even check my email for fear that someone was going to bash on me. So I hid behind large clothing, behind the walls of my house, and I hid inside the walls of my head.

I'M TIRED, JUST REALLY, REALLY TIRED OF THIS.

Curiosity was what destroyed me but it was also what was going to save me. It didn't leave me be, nagging at my heart.

"Look into it. Seek some help Ella. You're sick."

I responded back to its tugs.

"Please, I'm not sick. I got this! But I'll go ahead and look into it if it makes you shut up."

Soon I lost myself in reading up on how to break habits, the definition of an eating disorder, the psychology on the depressed mind, and other related topics such as the development of will power.

I began to search through all these topics and much more for answers as to what was really occurring inside me and at times I found myself searching for reasons why.

Each book told me the same shit as all the rest:

"You are not alone. You are not even immune to it. It does not matter your sex, your race, your age, it can develop inside anyone given the right situations or genetic makeup. Anywhere from 5-20% of those who suffer from an eating disorder will lose their lives to it. Don't let that be you. A full recovery is possible. Here's how..."

I read that shit over and over again. The same information being told to me, that I wasn't alone, it was okay to feel sad, confused, frustrated.

You're human. You'll get over this. It's nothing to be ashamed of.

BUT I DO HATE IT AND I AM TERRIBLY ASHAMED OF MYSELF.

I hated even googling 'bulimia' or 'how to recover from an eating disorder'. I hated how the once-loose sweatpants I had were now tight around my quadriceps and ass. As if my lower half wasn't big enough already, the binging has added at least ten pounds to my legs or so it felt. My arms had lost their solid definition and my teeth couldn't seem to get rid of the stomach acid on them at night when I lay down to rest.

I was also finding it harder to go out in public. People checked my body out and I could see their minds. I hated it all with so much passion that I began to consider the idea of taking anabolic steroids to lean me down and I thought about taking IGF-1 to heal me up fast.

But nothing seemed worth it and I left myself to cry in my sloppiness. Just the thought of cheating on my natural build and hard work with steroids caused me to stumble into another harsh reality, I didn't even know who I was anymore.

I just kept falling and it was exhausting.

My curiosity was still tapping on my shoulders and my eyes were still searching for comfort so I continued to spend my time with my eyes deep into addiction books and recovery books as I sat Indian style in the aisles of a local Barnes N' Nobles. I read up on steps on how to recover, what an eating disorder entails, how your friends and family can help you help yourself.

Am I alone? Will I ever be able to actually control this disorder? Can I change myself?

I scanned those books, making sure no one saw the titles of them. I checked to make sure that there was no one who knew me in the building.

And so I sat, I read, I took notes.

Curious.

WHAT IS BEING HEALTHY LIKE?

I stopped randomly in the middle of one book that told me to write down the worst moment I'd had with my eating disorder, and it got me thinking, I remembered almost dying.

Statistics show that about twenty percent of those who suffer from an eating disorder lose their lives to it and on one day particular, I almost found myself joining that percentage.

It was a typical start to my day, I awoke to a familiar stiff stomach, a dry mouth with the taste of stomach acid, and the thought that today was the day that I should start over. It was a new day and I got this.

However, once I got downstairs, I went blank and began to binge heavily on everything I saw early that morning. I don't remember where my parents had gone to that day, but I was left alone with the kitchen's familiar temptations and all the evil voices lurking inside my head.

I got this.

I walked from the fridge to pantry then to the freezer and all over again. I moved around stuffing my face with all kinds of shit, just straight up shit food.

HERE WE GO AGAIN, WEAKLING.

Saltines, cereal, cheese, ice cream, cottage cheese, peanut butter, almond butter, leftover noodles, frozen brownies, orange juice, chocolate milk, chips, deli meat, even carrots and raw vegetables entered my vacuum of a mouth.

WHAT HAVE I DONE?

I ate whatever I saw and I didn't stop until I felt the food in my throat yelling at me for mercy.

You're weak. You're so weak Ella!

Without much thought, I headed towards the drawer filled with silverware to pick up a long, smooth fork.

My purging forks.

My little helpers.

Have you ever just looked at a fork? I mean, *really* looked at it? Isn't it sort of silly looking? It's small handle acts as a lever for our hands to hold onto and at the end of it stands three or four sharp blades, ready to pierce our food. We often rely on this simple tool to give us our food, give us the energy we need, and give us satisfaction with each bite we take.

But as I look at a fork, I do not see such things, I do not receive such satisfaction nor do I use the fork to give me energy or to give me the food that I need. I have used this tool in such an abusive manner for so long, taking away such goodness from myself, that I only see it as a leverage to hell.

And it was in my left hand.

Fuck forks!

It was my fifth cycle to purge that day and I was having a difficult time getting the food to come up so I pulled out some tricks that I knew of and chugged a diet soda to help sizzle up the food.

WHAT THE ACTUAL FUCK, WON'T YOU JUST COME UP ALREADY, I NEED TO GET RID OF YOU.

I sat and waited as the force of liquid rushed down my throat and splurged into my incredibly full stomach. I took a moment to mentally prepare myself as I grasped the long fork in my left hand. It was always my left hand that held the fork.

I HATE YOU!

The worst part was always forcing the fork past my swollen throat glands, I could never seem to get it past them without scraping them open with the blades of the fork, causing more pain to emerge throughout my body.

I CAN'T STOP NOW, I ATE SO MUCH, THERE'S SO MUCH MORE, I'LL BE A FAILURE IF I DON'T DRY MYSELF OUT.

Bite your lip; swallow.

I dangled the fork, my tongue trying so hard to stop it, but I pushed past it.

Fuck you, fuck everything you stand for, fuck who you are, fuck who you were, fuck where you are, fuck this and fuck that.

The fork slid down into my throat and up came the burning acid along with a few chunks of what appeared to be brownies and oatmeal. That shit never tastes as good coming up by the way.

Slightly smiling now, I knew that my purging was back in business, I was getting my release and my sin was delivering itself to me. So I continued to perform my pathetic act next to the toilet.

Still holding onto the fork with my acid-covered fingers in my left hand, I slipped it back into my mouth and tipped my head back. The fork scraped its way past my tongue, my swollen glands, and into my throat. The acid on my fingers caused my grip to become nonexistent and before I knew it, I lost the fork.

I'M DONE.

Forget your life, your pain, your family, your friends, and your health.
Forget it.

Death was just outside my window and I looked at it straight in the eyes. He smiled at me and welcomed me.

"We've been waiting for you to give up Ella. To let others see you for who you truly are and just let it go. Let the pain go and join me, trust me, there is no pain here."

It slid a little more.

I'M GOING TO DIE. I'M GOING TO FUCKING DIE RIGHT HERE BY THIS DUMB TOILET WITH A FUCKING FORK IN MY MOUTH, HOW PATHETIC ARE YOU ELLA?

My head still cocked straight back, my eyes bulging from my face as tears streamed down my cheeks, the veins in my neck were just about to burst in fear, my breathing was now ceasing slowly, and my heart was almost stopping due to shock.

I'M GOING TO DIE. THIS IS IT.

The blades were digging into the back of my throat and I could feel the blood loosen it up as it gracefully progressed its way down.

IT WOULD BE EASY, YOU KNOW.

I think of my Mother.

I think of my Father.

I think of my Brothers.

I think of my Sister.

I think of my friends.

I think of those who support me.

I think of my life.

And I think of my death....

I imagined their faces, I imagined my Mother after a few days of wondering why I hadn't answered any of their calls from downstairs and as to why my truck was still in the driveway but I was nowhere to be seen.

I COULD END THIS PAIN RIGHT HERE AND JUST LET IT ALL GO.

Then I imagined what her face would be like when she saw me lying dead on the bathroom floor with my face ranging from shades of white to shades of purple due to the suffocation from the fork stuck in my throat. She'd pick up my dead-weighted body, as my hands that were once tightly gripped around my throat fall down to my side, she'd hold me close to her heart.. I could hear her cries. I didn't want her to see me like that. I didn't want anyone to see me like that.

I DON'T WANT TO DIE, I DON'T WANT TO DIE.

I hadn't moved a single muscle and although I was terrified of what would happen next, I decided to quickly reach back into my mouth to grab the end of the fork. Just as I touched it, I could feel its blades cut up the back of my throat more and it was now free to fall. My fingers scrambled in the small space of my throat, I felt the smooth edge of the metal.

There it is! Get it! Oh God I can't! Fuck! No wait! Oh my god I got it!

I now had the fork in my grip but I could still see death and it was still motioning me towards it. However, next to it I saw my family's faces.

I don't want this.

I don't know what I want.

I pulled the fork out of my mouth and with it came blood and acid that boiled through my teeth and spilt all over my shirt and body.

Within an instant of removing the fork from my throat, from saving my own life, I collapsed down to the ground and began to cry so hard to myself that I choked and quivered around the toilet.

Still gripping the fork in my left hand, I screamed, "I will never do this again!"

BUT I FUCKING NEED THIS.

I wish I could tell you that in that very moment I truly changed, that I decided that it was actually going to be my last time, and after looking death in the face that it would change me to become stronger and better, that it could cause me to rethink my actions.

But I was far too lost to even consider giving up and as much as I wish that was my turning point it wasn't.

I found myself next to the toilet two hours later, looking down at what appeared to be my only way of life. A toilet filled with bile and blood, a long fork in my left hand, my gut cramping, my body trembling, my mind collapsing, tears falling from my chin. This was my sick love affair and I didn't know how to stop the abuse.

Force that fork past your bleeding throat, your swollen, punctured glans, and the lack of enamel on your teeth. You are bulimia's little bitch.

I'll do whatever you demand of me.

TAKE ME, TAKE ME AWAY.

I repetitively told myself that I didn't have the dedication, the will power, the strength to resist these urges, to get that body I want, to reach greatness, so this was what I had to do, this was my justification.

Punishment is just another part of my habit, I didn't desire to feel good if I slipped up, this was my life and I was ruining it one binge at a time.

I desperately needed some sort of leverage with my problems and the fork in my left hand seemed to be my tool to another meaning of life.

What does leverage mean to you? According to the Oxford Dictionary, leverage when used as a noun is defined as: 'the exertion of force by means of a lever, or an object used in the manner of a lever' and when used as a verb, it means 'to use (something) to maximum advantage.'

Perhaps I used the invention of the fork to help simplify my life with to its maximum advantage. But instead of using properly, I complicated my life, my head, and blurred out the clear meaning of life by piercing my sensations with the end of the fork.

Although, the object ends there with its blades, it is also just another beginning to me. No matter how many times I looked at the tool in my left hand, I would forever feel the blood running down my throat and I would remember that even the simplest of things in life can become complicated.

Bite your lip; swallow.

This is not where I want to be.

GET AWAY FROM ME.

Darkness.

Death is easy, it is a full escape from yourself, your problems, and the world but it is never truly worth it to take your life when it's not your time.

I never tried to take my life intentionally nor did I ever give it too much thought but I won't lie, I did think about it.

My parents always talked about those who committed suicide as being selfish and weak and I didn't want to be seen that way by them or by anyone. The words we say to others can affect them whether we realize it or not, and it was the simple fact that my parents viewed suicide this way that made me opt out from ever trying it, even when I wanted it.

I can slightly remember the times when food was just food and a fork was just a fork to me, when I didn't look down at my plate and see carbohydrates, protein, and fats and analyze calories.

It didn't matter what I consumed, I was never phased by what entered my stomach, I didn't beat myself up for having some dessert with my family, for putting creamer in my coffee, and I could eat spaghetti without hesitation.

Those precious, simple moments are long gone for me now. I have forgotten what it's like to live and to just be since I began to have a constant worry about my daily life.

You forget what 'full' feels like, forget what food tastes like, you also don't know what it feels like to be neutral and healthy.

Either my throat was raw and sore from puking with my stomach in knots and my mouth dry from stomach acid or I felt so weak and hungry that all I could do was sleep my days away.

I truly hated myself. Some days I wished that something would take me away.

Perhaps that day I would get hit by a truck on my way to the gym crossing the bridge that's not far from home. Its impact would be so strong that my truck will roll off the walls and fall down to the ground where the grim reaper would be waiting for me.

That thought was where peace within myself was. The thought that death from my eating disorder was my only escape. I wanted to know what it was like to feel healthy. At that point, I was purely curious to know how I would leave this earth due to my depressing thoughts, and so I started to envision death as if it was a beautiful act of freedom for myself.

I couldn't even stand my own home because it had now become so tainted with my demons' ways. I hated my body and how I could never seem to fit into my clothes for extended periods of times due to my weight fluctuating so much. I also didn't feel worthy to be so many people's inspiration.

My demons waited for me ever so patiently in the back of my skull with their moldy hands drenched in pain, reaching outwards to the creases in my brain for any little chance that they could get to grasp ahold of me, to live through me and strangle me dry.

You're disgusting.

I was slowly killing myself but, in a very scary way, that was what made me Ella Anne, the girl who was unstoppable.

As hard as I fought the demands of my demons, I lost so many of my battles. I fell on my face, pathetically rolling around in my bed trying not to cry too loudly so that my parents wouldn't hear me. Maybe I was trying to drown myself in my tears.

I remembered a time when life was simpler. I missed it.

I missed a time when there wasn't a voice in my head making me fucking crazy, when I would just eat and be happy, when I wouldn't breakdown crying at night because the sadness inside me was so overwhelming that it pushed me to the breaking point.

I lived alone in misery. It seemed inevitable. It seemed like the right thing to do and I did it well. Oh hell yeah, I did it so well that I continued to win races, grow a bigger fan base by the day, gather sponsorships, snag interviews, and receive praise from my very own family.

Let's go back and review Erik Erikson's Stages of Psychosocial Development:

Stage 1: Trust vs. Distrust

Stage 2: Autonomy vs. Shame and doubt

Stage 3: Initiative vs. Guilt

Stage 4: Industry vs. Inferiority

Stage 5: Identity vs. Confusion.

Stage 6: Intimacy vs. Isolation.

Stage 7: Generativity vs. Stagnation

Stage 8: Integrity vs. Despair

Ultimately it's you vs. you and the main problem for me was that I didn't even know who I was and the war within me was confusing the hell out of me. I was fighting an unknown force that was attacking something that was also so misunderstood.

What gives?

My father is Cherokee Indian, so growing up I always read their legends and learned a lot from their teachings. One of my favorite legends is the legend of "Two Wolves" which is also known as "Grandfather Tells" or "The Wolf Within".

An old grandfather said to his grandson, who came to him with anger at a friend who had done him an injustice, "Let me tell you a story.

I too, at times, have felt a great hate for those that have taken so much, with no sorrow for what they do.

But hate wears you down, and does not hurt your enemy. It is like taking poison and wishing your enemy would die. I have struggled with these feelings many times." He continued, "It is as if there are two wolves inside me. One is good and does no harm. He lives in harmony with all around him, and does not take offense when no offense was intended. He will only fight when it is right to do so, and in the right way.

But the other wolf, ah! He is full of anger. The littlest thing will set him into a fit of temper. He fights everyone, all the time, for no reason. He cannot think because his anger and hate are so great. It is helpless anger, for his anger will change nothing.

Sometimes, it is hard to live with these two wolves inside me, for both of them try to dominate my spirit."

The boy looked intently into his Grandfather's eyes and asked, "Which one wins, Grandfather?"

The Grandfather smiled and quietly said, "The one I feed."

Bite the hand that feeds. Have you ever heard of that saying? Yeah, well, it was not just biting me, it was eating me! However, I don't think the war inside me was with wolves. I think the creatures within me were something untouchable, something we will never see during the daytime or even in our lifetime. We see them sometimes in movies, on cards, shirts, we even see them in our dreams. They're filled with magic and possess an undeniable amount of beauty. But also, they will always be known as forbidden and lost. The creatures that fight inside me are so rare that they don't even exist in this world.

They're unicorns.

I tried to make my life feel lighter by bringing humor to my crazy head. So I envisioned two unicorns fighting within me, one is full of all the evil just like the Grandfather speaks of. His skin drapes off his rotten bones, he snarls with blood dripping between his teeth, and nothing but anger flows through him. He tells me to self-destruct. While the other unicorn displays such beautiful strength, her skin glows with pure wisdom, and acceptance flows through her mane, she tells me to love myself.

Gosh darn it, these unicorns within me, they're so hungry.

You start to think of ways you could have prevented yourself from falling into this sick life. Wondering how and why you did this to yourself. You brew up ideas for your own personal preventions, recognize the bad behaviors you practiced back then, you see all the obvious signs. But it's too late, you can't go back in time and tell the old you to stop it, knock it off, you're going to ruin yourself because you already did. Now you're someone with an eating disorder for the rest of your life.

Let's look at some facts for a moment here and get some things straight. Eating disorders don't give a shit about who you are or what you do, they just come forth and take a hold of you. It doesn't matter if you're a female or a male, if you're an athlete or a business manager, if you're homosexual or heterosexual, or if you're Hispanic or European. It comes after you with a hunger.

Eating disorders are the leading mental disorder in mortality rates but generally most die due to heart failure, organ failure, malnutrition, or suicide.

I would have died by my very own hands, it would have been a tragic accident that happened just shortly after my twentieth birthday.

Soon after witnessing my own possible death, I finally realized that I did have an issue, that this wasn't right. I didn't know how to ask for help but I was fully aware that it was greatly needed. I couldn't go to bed crying any more for the desperate need to change. But I was not able to bestow the courage upon myself to make that change happen.

It just was not right.

July 2013: The death of my dog.

Brownie or Brown dog as I used to call her was a fat, 90 pound something chocolate lab who, in my opinion, resembled a plump sweet potato. My mother and I bought her from the side of the road in my freshman year of high school.

We originally got her for my oldest brother Tyler as an early birthday present and graduation gift. She went off to be with him for about two years while he finished college at Texas A&M University. After graduating Tyler went straight to the Navy, therefore Brownie came home to me.

She became my best friend. We went on long rucks together. We went swimming at the park. I fed her spoonfuls of peanut butter, and she slept in my bed every night with her obnoxious snoring. I loved the hell out of that dog and the day she left me was severely traumatizing.

I'll never forget her.

I had been going to physical therapy for my foot for quite some time now and I was finally able to walk without a boot but I had somehow managed to pull my back during this time.

I was still binging heavily, finding myself lost, having no clothes that fit me right, and deeply confused. I had this overwhelming sense of hatred for all things, because just two days previously a fork got stuck down my throat and I almost died.

I was trying hard to get back to a normal life, so that evening my friend Taylor came over to go for a hike by the river. Of course, I threw on a twenty pound weighted vest regardless of my back ache. I told myself "I might as well make this a little bit of a workout for myself, plus, I'm fat, I need to work it off somehow."

Brown dog, get in the truck!

Her fat little body hopped in. Her golden brown eyes glistened with happiness; that big pink tongue hung out of the side of her mouth and her tail wagged sporadically side to side then in circles.

I thought to myself "life is going to get better. You're okay Ella. Things could be much worse."

We started hiking that evening around 6:30pm and the temperatures hung around in the upper eighties. I had one Camelpak filled with water along with my weighted vest. We started off on the shaded part of the trail that snakes around the riverbed and goes up to the hills.

Time passed quickly and before we knew it, we had covered almost three miles. I looked back to see where Brown dog was at because her panting wasn't nickering in my ears anymore. I saw her standing there, looking drunk.

"Brownie?"

She looked at me, foam spilling out of her mouth. We shared a short glance at each other and then her eyes flickered into the back of her skull. She fell straight down to the ground and started rolling down the side of the hill.

It all felt fake. It was too surreal. My baby girl couldn't be doing this, not now.

I sprinted over to her just in time to catch her before she fell off the cliff-side. The weighted vest was digging into my traps, my lower back was already screaming in pain, my eyes full of concern. She was having a heat stroke.

My feet dug into the ground as I strained to lift her dead-weight body up the hill. I lost traction between the soft dirt and the tread on my shoes as I tried to climb up. My only thought at that moment was to get to the top of the hill or we were both going to die. My back muscles began to strain even more as I struggled to pull her up the hill. The tears started to fall from my eyes. I yelled over at Taylor who was standing at the edge of the trail with her hands over her mouth.

"Get my Camelpak! Get my freaking Camelpak! Dump the water on her! We need to cool her off right now!"

Brownie you're going to be okay.

My heart was panicking. I was hating myself inside for putting Brown dog in this position and just as quickly as she fell, she began to lose consciousness.

She started to die in my arms.

The river was too far from us and there wasn't any water left to cool her off with. We were three miles away from the truck, and Brownie's life was ticking away. I called my parents to inform them of the situation and our approximate location.

"Please hurry, it's now about 7:30pm and the sun is disappearing!"

Between my dog dying and my back killing me, I was at a loss for words and for the next forty minutes I attempted to carry Brownie home to safety.

Taylor wasn't strong enough to carry her, so she walked besides us wearing my weighted vest, her voice soft and calming.

"She's going to be okay. We'll laugh about this tomorrow morning."

I wanted to believe that I was dreaming a terrible nightmare.

I picked up Brown dog.

"I'm going to save you baby girl, don't worry."

I carried her as best as I could. We fell countless times and I dropped to my knees, screaming my head off in back pain.

GOD DAMNIT WHY NOW.

The tears came and went from my face. I wiped away the mud and sweat.

She's going to be okay, I got this.

I had to get her home so I continued to keep stumbling through the trails with her lifeless body. I carried her for about a mile until my back finally gave out on me and I fell to the ground with Brownie cradled in front of me. Her thick saliva covered my body as we fumbled down onto the ground together, and although we fell as one, she fell even farther than I did.

I looked up to the stars to see the night's sky now upon us. Where the hell are my parents?

The pain in my back was crippling me. I couldn't go any further carrying her, so we sat down on the trail and I petted her, sniffling up my tears. I tried to coax her as we waited on the trail for my parents to arrive. The time passed slowly and my heart was sinking further and further by the second.

When my parents finally reach us, it was 9:45pm. They brought a cot and a pack filled with ice cold water and towels. We quickly put the cold water all over Brownie and draped the drenched towels around her chest. She was motionless by then, laying limp on the ground. We picked her up and put her onto the cot so that the four of us could carry her home. We each grabbed hold of a corner of the cot and began to hike back.

We got this.

The trek back was filled with an uneasy amount of silence. We did not speak a word as we struggled up and down the trails circling the hillside then ventured down to the riverbed.

Brownie started to have out of control diarrhea. She even attempted to get up and so we found ourselves constantly having to readjust. My parents hadn't brought any source of light so we used the screens from our cell phones as guidance, attracting more bugs than we'd have liked.

We hustled through the trails together, hoping to save my best friend.

It took us about an hour and a half to get back to the truck. As soon as we reached it, we loaded up and rushed home to get brownie out. Once we arrived home, I picked up my best friend's lifeless body and stood her up on the driveway only to catch her into my arms as she fell.

I started to hose her off with cold water. It was now midnight and the darkness of the night was magnifying by the seconds. She was no longer responsive to my voice, her eyes didn't glisten anymore, and her panting was now gone.

My baby girl.

My best friend.

That night Brown dog died after suffering from a heart attack along with her heat stroke.

I spent the next day laying in my bed with a swollen face, a broken heart, and a back that wouldn't allow me to move. Everything hurt me, I missed my dog already, I felt as if it was my fault and I couldn't even keep my emotions together enough to go out in public. So I spent the entire day mourning the death of my best friend.

Realizing that I no longer had her tubby, short frame, that smiling face, and tennis ball loving presence by my side anymore, freaked me out. The voices started to get dangerously loud inside my head. I was falling deeper into this negative pool of despair, I couldn't swim well nor did I have any of my ducky floaties handy.

I was going to drown in this sorrow.

Wadding in this pool of negativity, all of these new fears exposed themselves to me. I feared sleeping without her cuddled next to me in bed. I feared not being able to talk to her about my issues anymore. I no longer had the privilege of waking up to her sweet kisses. No more cruising in the truck, and no more of our long walks through the woods together.

Brown dog was the only one I ever told about my bad eating habits. I used to tell her all the time.

"I think I have an eating disorder."

Then she was gone, and I had no one to talk to.

That night I was exhausted from crying. Sleep should have been easy for me but I could not seem to bear the thought of sleeping alone. So after my parents went to bed that night, I ventured down to the kitchen.

When I opened the silverware drawer that night to get a spoon, I saw it. I saw my heartache lying next to the spoons and for a split second I stared down at them, took a moment to feel my heart bleed out, I just couldn't escape it. My heart was incredibly broken. I used to be just a girl living freely but it seemed as though I couldn't be that anymore.

First, I made a huge bowl of ice cream that was loaded with chocolate chips, caramel, almonds, crumbled cookies, and I plastered the top of it with some thick whipped cream. It was a beautiful bowl of goodness.

Instead of pacing around the kitchen, I actually sat down to enjoy it and as I sat there pitifully in the silence I began to realize just how alone I truly was.

At first I couldn't eat it. I was sick to the stomach from crying, but as soon as the ice cream touched my tongue, I went numb inside.

It was time to self-destruct.

I was submerged in the waters even more now. I was being taken away by the current and just like that, I stopped trying to paddle against it. I didn't fight the pull anymore and let myself drift into the sea's seemingly never-ending coastline.

My dog had left my side at such a fragile time in my life. It couldn't have been a worse time for me to be forced to be alone.

Depression took over my life after her death and I didn't fight it too much. It was easy to let go when you felt as if you had nothing left. So there went my life. Nights blended into mornings and mornings blended into evenings. I was hidden away inside my home where I had no real motivation and no desire to go outside.

And so the egocentric binging side of me gets its wishes of self-destruction completely.

Some days got so intense, that I couldn't even try to go to the gym because I was too full of food to move, and my back hurt too much for me to bear, so it was an easy excuse for me to lay down and sleep.

I called to make fake excuses about why I couldn't go to physical therapy so that instead I could go and sit down at the river where my dog died. There I would contemplate my life, and sit there with a stiff gut watching the tall grass just be as it moved with the wind. I envied that grass.

Enjoy my defeat.

Not long after Brown dog left my life I had to attend more fitness expos. I put on more fake fronts, hid more of my hurt and met so many more wonderful fans. I greeted them with hugs and smiles, but inside I was on the verge of tears throughout every encounter I had. The majority of them looked at me in the eyes and I could feel their love. But some were so easy to read, I could look straight through their eyes and see the backs of their skulls.

"Wow, look how heavy Ella Kociuba's gotten."

WHAT AM I DOING WITH MY LIFE, WHY AM I HERE?

I was so sick during that time that I wanted to break down in front of people as they approached me. I envisioned grabbing their shirts as I fell to my knees.

"Please for the love of all things holy… you have no idea what's going on with me, I need your help!"

But I couldn't, I just couldn't express myself, not there, not then. So I stood there awkwardly, trying to forget that I was hurting inside. I hid my sadness so that it wouldn't rub off onto those around me.

I didn't want to be a negative Nancy, so I told myself to "suck it up buttercup". I put on an act as if I was alright.

It's cool, I'm Ella Anne Kociuba. It's cool.

No. I'm not alright and I'm not cool with it.

I need some serious help.

For the first time in my life, I was in a war that I could not battle out alone, nor did I have to, and so I reached my hands out.

I could not stomach the thought of actually opening up about my bulimia to my family or my friends yet, so I got in touch with a nutritionist by the name of Layne Norton. With his guidance I began to climb back up hill.

He introduced me into the world of flexible dieting and I slowly got rid of my strict diets of white fish, no oiled vegetables, complex carbs, and the occasional cheat meals (which, honestly, ended up becoming a cheat day).

My approach to nutrition changed completely and it started to get more relaxed. I realized that I could eat foods like cookies, pop-tarts, ice cream, cheeseburgers, and even chicken with oil and not feel guilty or shameful. I could keep things in moderation.

Becoming well felt weird to me. Healthy was an odd feeling, but sanity felt real nice to me and with this new diet of macronutrient counting, I started to find it.

My physique slowly started to slim back down. My deltoids rounded off, the vascularity returned to my arms, my legs got harder, and my back muscles became hypertonic with my leanness.

I was a hardbody again. I was looking like the Ella I knew. Smiles commenced nonstop. More importantly, my binges started to fade and my mind seemed to become lighter with each day that passed.

I found happiness with my life again.

I was feeling like Ella Anne Kociuba.

There was a light at the end of the tunnel and my face was submerged in its rays. So close, yet so far away. My dreams. My sanity. I could see it all at the end of that tunnel thanks to Layne Norton's guidance and my very own decision to try to help myself.

Roller coasters go up and down and right now I believed that I'd cured myself but I still hadn't received the help that I really needed, even though I felt as if that was it. So I moved on with the thought that I was getting better, that I was recovering from my bulimia and that I would get over it.

Over it.

At the end of August, 2013 I was finally released and declared healthy enough from my foot injury to return to some light running. The endorphins from the word of my good health alone was enough to make me elated. A smile from ear to ear settled onto my face. Health was coming my way again… Or so I thought.

I was somewhat healthy in terms of my bulimia, I was working with my nutritionist, and I had my eyes set on next year's season. I follow a return-to-running program given to me by my physical therapist. It was more of a 'fat-loss grandma plan' by my definitions, but regardless of how lame I saw it, I bit the bullet and followed its simple guidelines.

Three weeks of slow jogging faded past me and on one morning, I laced up my shoes to pace out an easy five miles. As I jogged the trail path that morning, everything seemed to be alright until mile four. The same foot began to throb violently in sharp pulses, in a different spot than last time, and it quickly crippled me down into a walk. A pathetic limping walk.

Fuck fuck fuck fuck fuck fuck FUCK.

Was it really happening... Again?

I limped myself back to my truck, my eyes filled with anger and my mind driving straight into a huge pool of negativity. I called my doctor the next day and three days later got x-rays done.

"In three weeks," he said, "we will see if it is a stress fracture or just some major swelling in your metatarsal."

Three weeks come and go and even with my high spirits, I knew in the back of my mind that it wasn't something as small as "just some swelling". My foot disabled my everyday activities and even throbbed throughout the night. I could feel it in the bone but I kept thinking to myself that perhaps it was not the case, perhaps it was something small, perhaps I was just being a big baby...

Perhaps, perhaps, perhaps...

September 18th, 2013.

As I impatiently waited for the doctor, the nurse came in and pulled up the images on the computer. My eyes yearned out of the side of my head to get a peek at them. I saw a huge block of bone that obviously was out of place, I could feel the warmth develop underneath my eyes.

"I regret this."

Shit.

Sure enough, it was a stress fracture. My heart sank and I burst into tears when he told me. All I could think of was the pressure to perform, the contracts, my sponsors. I felt so unworthy of them all.

Here I was, a broken, run-down athlete at the age of twenty.

Injury after injury, battling it one after another, taking a punch and a kick in the privates...

GET ME AWAY FROM HERE.

"Your body is really going through the ringer."

Yea, NO SHIT. So is my mind. At least I think I still have one.

I went to my truck and cried my heart out once again in the very same parking lot filled with old people wobbling their way to doctor visits and eye appointments nearby.

Where's my break? Where's my break?

Battle after battle. What more must I endure?

Oh wait, my body, it's breaking.

There are two kinds of reaction you get from sadness, in my opinion. The first one is where you get so upset that you get a huge appetite and go towards food to fix your aches. The other is when you cry so hard, that even the thought of the best slice of your favorite cake in the world seems disgusting and there is no hunger inside you.

This was where I was at, I had no hunger, I had no hope.

I blasted Florence and The Machine so loudly that it vibrated the floor and the walls of my room. I laid down on the ground and grabbed the closest item to me, which was some dirty laundry. I cradled it against my stomach as I felt the eerie yet beautiful notes flow through my body.

The tears stopped but the ache proceeded as I laid there... My mind went numb as I drifted into sleep.

Darkness.

My lack of hunger quickly turned into an impulse to act on my emotions and I was back to the cabinets, the fridge, to the damn crackers, cereal, cheese, yogurt, bread, tortillas, peanut butter stuffing craze. I was back to binging and even back to practicing some purging cause I couldn't stand the shame of the stiff stomach I always developed after a matter of minutes. I even took more laxatives again.

I CAN'T WORKOUT WHAT AM I SUPPOSED TO DO HERE.

The fact that I had slipped up again killed me inside. I felt like such a failure.

"Bulimia, oh how forever haunting you are."

Give me mud. Give me scars.

Two days after I was told about the shattered bones in my foot, my phone rang. It was my athlete director from Spartan Race calling.

"Hi Ella, are you in a boot?"

"No."

"Are you in a cast?"

"No."

"Are you in crutches or anything of the like?"

"No. What is this about?"

The request that filled my ears in that very moment immediately caused my stomach to draw in and it felt as if my heart was getting poked with a hot metal rod while my lungs flared for air. I tried to grasp a hold of the new chills settling within me. I wanted to decline at first, but for reasons unknown I agreed to their offer and accepted my fate of being a product.

What was asked of me was to make a 'fake start' in the championship race held in Killington, Vermont and tell the cameras that I had to quit because... Well, because my foot hurts.

I was told that it would be better if I could make sure that I cried in front of the cameras because that would be great media exposure.

'Used' wasn't the only word I would use to describe my feelings at that point, but it was one of the first things that come to mind.

"Kill me." I thought, "This is not right."

I didn't tell them that my foot was actually stress fractured in two places and just took their plane tickets to Vermont.

I was filled with mixed emotions as I came off the plane to see the familiar faces, familiar land marks, and feel familiar feelings. This place would always have a huge part of my heart.

Oh, Vermont. The memories, the nightmares, you have so much of me.

This trip ended up being a memory I could just store away and observe through the glass wall like it was some sort of toxic chemical.

Wouldja just look at it? Look at how rotten that memory is and observe its powerful ache that embarks on my mind.

I came to Vermont with a weird head and I left with an even weirder head on my shoulders. My head didn't want to take any more abuse. I felt as if I was about to explode from my own self-induced labors and life's demands.

I watched as so many of my fellow competitors and friends raced in an event that I had been looking forward to for a year. I sort of disliked them at that moment. I saw their health and wondered why I could never actually feel like that and deep down inside me the war raged, so I kept on denying the obvious.

Buy I knew why, it was because I was my biggest burden.

People approached me, took pictures with me, and then asked me the most dreaded questions.

"Why aren't you out there competing?"

Or they'd tell me "You're going to win today."

I'd bashfully smile and look down. Trying to hide my sadness, a small chuckle would escape my lips.

"Yeah, no.. I'm not competing this weekend."

"You're hurt again? Jeeze."

I'm pathetic, I know.

Can I just go home already?

My interview with NBC was canceled due to my injuries. So they looked over at the other athletes who were able to compete and I was forgotten, I was sent to the curbside. I nodded my head in such despair as I observed others doing all the things I once did and once dreamt of, and be the greatness that I once was.

What is life?

So I was left to wander aimlessly on that Friday evening. I didn't even know what to do with my hands, literally. I ate the food given out at the feast and talked amongst others like everything was alright, but it certainly was not.

I didn't like that taste in my heart. It was disgusting.

I secretly binged all weekend in my bunk bed at the ski cabin they put us up in, finding myself crying randomly throughout the day and the nights that I spent there.

There was little to zero cell service. I'd eaten five Quest Bars, the dry cereal I had packed for my trip and some candy that I snuck from my friend's bag.

Bulimia often made me turn into a real sneaky person. I'd steal food and hide it my pockets and my bags, so that I could binge on it later. I'd creepily wiggle my fingers with pride as I snuck around taking just enough food so that no one would notice.

"Yes, I got you cookies, you're mine."

After binging some, I stepped outside and tried to call my mom, but I couldn't get a connection out to call her and so I sat in the cold to cry by myself. Although I didn't know what exactly I was going to say to her, all I knew is I that needed to hear her voice and I needed to cry.

I felt so determined to turn myself around at that point in my life because the aches that throbbed throughout my body, my mind, and my spirit were just not worth it. They were taking the best of me, and I was so tired of them all.

My trip shed some light on the reality of being an athlete and it finally became clear to me that I was not a person to some, I was more of a product, and I absolutely hated it.

Hate is a strong word, but I truly do mean it here.

Something inside me, whether it was the hurt or the pure hatred for the way I felt urged me to hit the trails harder, lift the weights harder, and train my mind to grow even harder.

The exhaustion of constantly fighting was taking a huge toll with everything about me. Everything I felt, and everything I did was now ruined.

Determination is a word we can use here, but it also felt more like redemption and hey, they say revenge is best served on a golden platter.

I am as wise as the decaying bones in the wilderness.

Cover me in dirt, there's so much truth here.

I am as free as the mangled flesh flowing from the dead.

Bury me with dirt, I am that balance between lost and losing.

As bitter as I felt and sounded, I actually got over the fact that I was not number one, I was not the Holy Grail. I was not that nineteen year old phenomenon anymore and I found peace with it.

I had been dreaming of coming back to the racing field and showing them what was up.

"Hey, remember my punk ass? YEAH, well I'm back! Look at my shredded body, see how fast and strong I am? How do you like me now?"

I had it all planned out and it was going to be magical, like a cheetah riding a unicorn. But I suddenly lost passion for that idea, it all seemed to be really unimpressive (notice that I have this feeling back into my life). It was lame, I lacked the motivation to charge back. Then I felt it. The feeling of being burnt out.

Instead of coming back super strong in the obstacle racing field, I began to watch so many other athletes take titles, win the races I used to conquer, and get famous with their trophies, all while I struggled with my eating disorder on the sidelines.

Even though I should have taken another three to four months to train so that I could get back into competition shape, I was impatient and so I returned to the field in February of 2014 to compete.

I was in a weird condition, aesthetically looking decent but mentally destroyed. I put on fake smiles, an act of happiness for so many others.

I told them "I'm much healthier now and back to compete!" But it was just an act and all I really wanted to do was go home and be alone. There, I could cover myself under my bed sheets, listen to Citizen Cope, moan about the stomach ache erupting in my guts, write in my journal "this is the last time, I'm tired of this", bawl my eyes out with the confusion in my head, and bury myself into the frustrating feeling of being a burden to myself and not knowing how to stop it.

I just wanted to be alone, depression wanted me to be alone.

CHAPTER 4
DARKNESS

What it takes is your everything

But are you willing to give that all away.

When I tried to talk to someone about my problems, I felt like a chair that was placed off to the side of the room at some bitchin' party. The only people who came over to me were the overweight and elderly, and they did not care to ask how I was doing. Instead they came to just use me, to sit down on me. I was trapped in the corner of this confusing party going unnoticed and crushed underneath a burden I did not know how to function with. It was heavy and I felt old within myself.

I couldn't be breaking down already!

Suddenly, I didn't know how to speak and so I just sat in silence and let those around me use me for their betterment when really, I was in such great need of their help.

It is not that I feared judgment towards me or even anticipated those who may have strayed away from my exposure to such struggles. But I hesitated to open up and, even more than that, I was afraid of what I would become after I did so.

I was afraid that the exposure of my darkness would change me. When I was no longer in hiding, quiet and 'alone', just who would I become? I was already aware that people would look at me and not only would they know of my struggles, they would actually see them. They would not just see my physical struggles but they would also get some insight on the fight inside my head, the one which terrified the hell out of me.

For me, "Help me" was one of the hardest things to say, along with "I love you" and "I'm sorry". Opening up about my eating disorder sort of felt like a HUGE "I'm sorry, help me."

Year 2014 rolled around and life was looking promising yet again.

I returned back to the racing circuit with even more eyes upon my shaved, leopard spotted head and I moved around with even more hunger inside my soul than in the years before.

In February, I entered into my first event, Extreme Nation, with a team of four and we came out in first place. I wasn't too happy with my own performance but looked at it as a bench mark.

Things could only go up from there.

A couple of weeks after competing over in Florida, I travelled off to compete in Southern California in another team event called Superhero Scramble. The team that I was part of came in second place.

It appeared from the outside looking in that I was on my way back and settling into my groove with ease. But that was not the case whatsoever. I was struggling with body image issues. My chronic back pain was more obnoxious than usual, and it seemed to me that I just sucked at everything.

I somewhat got my shit together and started living my days without my eating disorder.

In March, not long after stepping back into my competitions, my brother Casey, my second oldest sibling who I always looked up to, graduated from Marine OCS School.

My family and I went up to Quantico, Virginia to watch his ceremony with great pride in the miserable cold temperatures.

For some odd reason, I couldn't help but feel sadness swell over me and I became lost in confusion as to why it was there.

Here was my beautiful family and I, watching my brother doing great things. Why was I sad?

Unfortunately, the love around me was not enough to prevent me from falling down on my face.

And so I fell. Smack!

It had been awhile since I'd seriously relapsed into a binge and purge cycle. But on that very night, I fell back into the whirlpool of self-doubt. Back into an out of control binge, I found myself drinking a chocolate smoothie from Starbucks and eating bags of salted kettle chips and four boxes of girl scout cookies on our flight back home to the warmth of Texas.

My once lean belly turned into a huge bloated basketball. I looked pregnant.

Ah, t-shirt don't touch my skin. Don't feel my pain.

I get asked questions all the time.

"Why did you open up about your eating disorder?"

"What made you open up about your bulimia?"

"Weren't you scared of people judging you, hating you, making fun of you, or anything like that?"

It wasn't any one thing in particular that made me do it. It was a simple moment for me really, no one said anything to me to make me come out. Nothing dramatic happened except my own head processing my pain and deciding that change needed to happen. It just felt right.

Needless to say, I was simply tired of hurting and feeling so alone in my sorrow.

What did happen was that I simply looked at my surroundings. I had a purpose. I scanned the plane on our way home, with my stomach bulging, my legs becoming jet lagged, my fingers swollen.

I looked over at an elderly woman sitting next to me sleeping with her mouth slightly slit open, her navy-blue skirt and silky white top carefully fitted onto her tiny frame. I saw the life within her and I found myself envious of her contentment. I observed her in the most non-creepy way as she quietly slept with the thin air from the plane's vents streaming into her lungs. From what I could tell, she appeared to be healthy, she also appeared to be about eighty-two years old.

I WANT THAT.

I wanted to live a long, beautiful, healthy life where one day I fell asleep wearing my JC Penny outfit on a plane. I wanted to have no worries, to love my life and to be healthy.

Deep down, I knew that, if I continued on that route, I would never reach eighty-two. Even if I did, I wouldn't be as content as the woman next to me.

The thought of living so unhappily made my heart hurt something great, so I began to write. I wrote my heart out and as soon as the plane landed, I knew what needed to be done.

I needed to publish this online for all to see.

When we finally got to our house, late that night, I ran upstairs to rewrite everything onto my website's blog. Just before clicking 'publish', I wiped away my tears to take a moment to listen to the silence that lurked in my room. I knew there was this weight on my shoulders and I was about to let some of it go. Shit, I was so ready for the release to happen that it hurt just knowing that I was moments away. I wanted nothing more than to be healthy and content with myself.

WHAT HAVE I DONE?

Click.

The 'world' can see it now.

The 'world' will know ME now.

I broke into the biggest cry. My body seemed to shut down due to the explosive body shakes and the compulsive choking from my unforgiving tears that drowned out the voices in my head.

I had just ripped off a scab. I didn't recognize any of these emotions. I couldn't tell if I felt okay or not yet.

The following is taken from my online blog which was edited some, but I figured that my words written a few days after my announcement would be better than rewriting my mind's aches:

Fresh Scabs: 3/18/2014

What is the purpose of a scab?

To my understanding a scab is there to protect the outside from getting in, to isolate the injury in attempts to heal itself. It is a layer of protection, a layer to hide something, a layer that provides security. And there was a scab that hid me from the world and on this very day, I ripped it open for everyone to see.

Look at me, I struggle.

And boy did I just rip off one of the biggest scabs that I have ever received. But this scab was poisonous, it covered my heart, my mind, my soul, and my life. Just as blood runs out of a wound so did my emotions the day after telling the world 'I struggle with bulimia'. I find myself lost down by the river with such a swollen face that I can't even breathe correctly. I laid there in the middle of a valley with my weighted vest rubbing into the side of my neck, the grass irritating my skin, small ants biting at my ankles, and my water pack jamming into the creases of my armpits. With my cell phone in my hands, I begin to read. I read emails upon emails, text messages, tweets, messages, all other social media outlets, I read them all. All of the incredibly inspiring, supportive, and loving things people are telling me and I am so overwhelmed. More tears.

How could I even have tears at this point?

Let's back track to that night, Sunday night. I had just finished binging on whatever shit was out in front of me, the voices were so loud at this point that I became numb and lost control. I had been doing so well for so long. However, one battle was won and that was the urge to purge the food. But I was still left with a gut raging in pain.

Where is my greatness? Where is my strength?

A few moments pass after the confusion and I grow aggressive in my mind. I begin to self-doubt myself and grow hatred. I hate all the things. I've come so far. However, I didn't let it consume me and I swallowed the pain, the negativity and I wipe away my tears, and went straight to my laptop. I don't want to struggle anymore. I don't want to do this anymore. I don't want anyone else to feel like I feel. And so... I began to write.

I didn't give too much detail into my darkness for there are so many terrible stories about the struggles with my demons, some of which I might share much later on but for now I kept it simple. I put it out there. Raw, pure, and honest, I was ripping my scabs away. I sat for a moment after it was written and read it. And read it again. And again. And again. This was my life.

Click.

And just like that weight begins to come off my shoulders. Although, I do not feel better immediately. My tears are so heavy that I am drowning as I cuddle in my bed, stuffed animals surrounding me and the silence of the night filling the room. I cry all night and fall asleep only to wake up immediately with more tears. It's six a.m. and my day must begin. I look over at my phone and it is flooded with messages and texts. I open a few and I can't even handle it, these emotions are so demanding. It wanted all of me. And so, I let it have me. I let the tears pour down my face. I let my body shake in misery. I want to be present. I want to embrace this. I don't have the guts to look at the rest of the messages and so I head to massage school. But first, I send my mother a text to the link of my blog. And all I write is 'I love you'. She doesn't know it yet, she doesn't even have a clue and that makes me terrified. The whole drive there I suffer through tears. I feel like everyone knows now, even the random man standing on the sidewalk in the cold morning waiting for the bus knows it. I get to school and wait outside for my face to dry up and just as soon as class is supposed to start, I find a seat in the back of the room to sit with my face in my hands. I'm usually loud and vibrant. And here I was, quiet and timid.

We have an exam today and for every big exam we do we have a tradition of getting up in front of the class as a group and doing silly movements to help relax and get ready for the test. I stand there with my lips quivering, my eyes darting at everyone else's glances, my legs seem to tremble, and my arms. I don't know what to do with them so I begin to hide my face for I can feel the tears coming. When everyone goes to their seats my professor calls my name and I approach him, "Do you need to wait to take the test?" I can't even talk and I just look back at him. My face swelling, my eyes bloodshot, and then boom. I start to perform the choking cry. I am such a mess. He takes me outside of the classroom and just rubs my back and I cry. I cry like a little girl that I am. I cry so hard that I cause the whole table to shake. I am passed embarrassment of my tears now because for the first time I am free. I am free of a burden that was literally killing me from the inside out. I had never really told anyone and now I just told 'the world'.

I am taken to my professor's room and for the next two hours I lay on the ground crying, cuddling a blanket with Kleenex bundled up in one hand and the other covering my eyes. When finally my mind becomes quiet and my heart is still enough that I drift into a deep sleep and am awaken only to be told I have to sit in on the CPR class, so I get up and adjust myself. I can hardly recognize my face when I look in the mirror, it looks as if I have elephantiasis. I try to bring humor to myself and I whisper, 'let's do this bitch'.

I sit for the next two hours holding back more emotions. I avoid eye contact at all costs and I awkwardly leave class in a hurry to head home. I get home and make the simplest of simple foods as I can. I've cried so much that I don't even have an appetite but I know I should eat, so I eat some egg whites and oatmeal. I then throw on my weighted vest and head to the river. I want to get lost only so I can find myself again.

This is where I am for the next five hours. I hike out about five miles. I find a log and I pick it up. This is my burden. I carry it, its weight not distributed correctly and it's splinters dig into the back of my neck as I carry it over my shoulders. For some reason the sharpness of the wood splinting into my skin does not affect me. This pain, I control. I walk onward into the warm sun until I find another log. This one is much heavier and in my mind I know he's my darkness. I pick the other log up and for the next forty minutes or so I carry both the logs. At some points I get so frustrated, I want to drop them both and say 'fuck you and all that you are'. But I don't, I pick the logs back up because this place on earth is not where they belong. I know when these burdens are done and where I should put them. I've never seen the place but I know it when I get there. When the time does come, I drop the logs and look down at them. These are my struggles and I am leaving you. This is my weakness, this was my life. And I am leaving that part of me behind. Nonetheless, these fresh new scrapes on my neck and biceps are a reminder. A reminder that even though I carried these logs, these struggles for a short period of time, they will always be a part of me somehow.

I finally get to a place where the trees tell me it's time to rest. I find a valley and I collapse onto the ground. And this is where you find me. I am now reading messages upon messages. So many heartaches, so many thank you's, I try to screenshot them all. I try to remember them all. Their names, their scars. I want to thank you. I want to hug you. My body is filled with so much love, support, and encouragement from so many strangers, friends, fans, and family that I don't think about my pain anymore. I find such silence in this moment that I cry now because of happiness. I fall asleep again. An hour passes by and I wake up extremely calm. Dried tears crack on my face as I squint towards the fading sun, perhaps it's time for me to head home. I look back at my phone and see I have a missed call from my mother. My gut drops. I need to talk with her. I need to hug her but I am still so scared and I don't know why.

The path home is one that is not dug into the earth, it is my own and I travel through it with such peace that even the stickers digging into my feet through my shoes don't bother me. I am smiling and grinning, touching the tall grass as I pass. Looking at the nature around me as I travel home, I cannot help but think, this greatness of pain is such a blessing, I am going to become stronger with each step and I was making damn sure of it. I know that I am not done crying for the day but at this moment I do feel the freedom. I do feel the release of my demons and I am present in this moment. For this is the moment I have ached for.

The talk with my mother is one that brightens my soul and eases more of my pain. It was such a weak moment for me as I told her about my struggles. Especially about how this Thanksgiving was the first Thanksgiving in three years where I was truly happy. So happy that I didn't binge and hide from everyone to go purge, that I was finally able to be fully present with my family. My mind wasn't hurting or stressing out about food. The pain I saw in her eyes made me cringe, she had no idea and that made me feel sorrowful. All I can do is tell her I love her and our hug at that moment was something so... breathtaking. Her love radiated out of her touch and I just collapsed into her arms.

Freedom.

More stories come to my email, Facebook, Twitter, Instagram, Tumblr, and my blog. I read them all with such big tears and I am saddened about how many other beautiful people also share my pain, but so grateful that I ripped off that scab to let the blood violently pour out from my life damaging wound. So many people tell me I'm brave and that I am strong, but at this moment I do not feel it. I hate seeing my name next to the word bulimia, when I first read the words together in the same sentence it made me cringe, it made me feel regret and embarrassment. Those shouldn't be together, I say, that's not me. Why did I tell everyone my secret? And then I keep reading the messages, I keep feeling the weight come off my shoulders as I read life changing moments, I read mindset alterations, and the thank you's. Oh the thank you's, if only I could tell each and every one of you in person how much it means to me, I would and perhaps one day I will. And of course, hug the shit out of you. If my story can touch, help, and change thousands of lives for the better than I am completely okay with feeling so vulnerable momentarily. This is why. This is why I shared my pain so that you don't have to feel it. So that you know you're not alone, that we all have flaws, and that we can all be vulnerable… Admitting to a flaw does not make you weak, denying them and avoiding the chance to change your life for the better does. I then feel the bravery. I then feel the strength as the blood from my wound begins to slow down. And as blunt and simple as I can say it, it is what it is and the time has come for my wounds to heal, for me to rise up, and to overcome this.

I have now ripped off an old scab, one of which was infected. While these next few days the blood from my wounds may gush out sporadically but it will soon scab over and this time the scab will be different. This scab will heal me instead of damage me.

From the bottom of my heart, I thank you.

Honestly, I didn't expect to get so much love from my 'coming out' with my eating disorder. Every day I had what seemed like hundreds of people reaching out their hands to me, sharing their own stories, telling me that I saved them, giving me their shoulders to cry on whether it was virtually or literally.

I actually printed off every single email that I received and put them into a binder, so that perhaps one day I can reach back out to everyone and thank them too.

The amount of support I received overwhelmed me in the greatest way possible, the feeling of a heart swollen with the selfless love from strangers is enough to make you cry and I didn't have an issue showing it.

Pouring out my three years of emotions seemed to last for a solid two weeks and it was a difficult realization for me to accept that I am now known for this issue.

I entered the gym and hid my face. I cried in between each set. I was at a loss for strength or even words.

In class I did not speak of my sad face, my problems. When I was at home I avoided the kitchen and I avoided my parents. Not once did I dare to go out with any of my friends. I avoided them too so that I could be alone.

I DON'T WANT TO TALK ABOUT IT RIGHT NOW. WHAT IS THERE TO BE SAID?

People seemed to watch me cry everywhere I went. My close friends heard nothing but my voicemail, and I sat at the dinner table suffocating in silence as my mother rubbed her hands on my back at night without knowing what to say to me.

I was so torn up inside that I couldn't even say a word either. Silence was falling upon my shoulders and it was humiliating for me to be so trapped. Every day after class, I found myself escaping out to the river down the road to get lost for hours, with nothing but a weighted vest secured tightly around my frame and a water bladder with yesterday's water left in it.

I didn't need much, just my mind, I wanted to get lost so that I could find myself. So in an attempt to let go of my pain, I wandered through the park's lands with no intentions of going home. Maybe I'd just quit life and live in the woods, I knew how to but never committed to the idea.

I ended up going home to sit and soak in my bubble bath. I was too tired to cry so I just sat there in silence observing the foam in my hands, the soap suds that were delicately placed on my stomach and legs while some of it was slowly sliding off my nipples.

Why can't I love my body?

I was truly convinced that everyone around me knew my dirty secret even if they didn't even actually know who I was.

When I went to buy energy drinks at the gas station after class, I felt like the women at the Seven Eleven knew that I was 'that girl with the eating disorder'. Even the homeless man on the corner of Anderson Mill, with his matrix looking coat knew it as I drove past him.

When I was in class I was uncomfortably aware that my classmates were curious as to why I cried.

When I entered the gym, the trainers looked at me with sad, worried eyes.

All those eyes were driving me insane. I didn't know if I was going to be able to find peace with being so vulnerable.

Hey everyone, you want a photo?

The thoughts of people judging me crept around me like a heavy fog. I was not sure that I liked being known for this anymore.

"Ella Kociuba opens up about her dark secret with her eating disorder."

Oh how odd it is to read about yourself online.

The temptation of evil had its chains around my throat dragging me through the dirt, laughing at me.

I got you, you don't got this.

But I'm a fighter, that's what I've learned to do.

Fight the good fight.

One of the worst things I heard after telling everyone I had this issue was when my mother, with her bloodshot, watery eyes, her dirty blonde hair swooping around her sweet face, looked at me in such pain and told me "I'm so sorry I wasn't there for you. I can't help but think, where was I?"

I tried to reassure her that there was no way she could have known. I hid it. I didn't want her to know because I wanted to believe that I could take care of myself. I really did at times.

Regardless of my stubborn head, I could recall trying to talk to her a few times. I would look up at her from the kitchen island and say, with a shameful smile, "Mom, I can't stop eating". But I was too ashamed of myself to actually ever say it. I literally felt as if I was trapped within myself. She'd laugh, smile, and tell me "I know neither can I."

"But no mom really, like it's bad."

I ended up just giving up on the thought of telling her that I was bulimic and continued to tell myself that I can do this, I got this.

YOU'RE ELLA ANNE KOCIUBA, YOU GOT THIS.

There are some things that you'll never understand in life and one of them might be something you have within you, bulimia is mine.

There was no need to try to find the justification for it, it would only lead to disappointment and therefore instead of trying to find out all the reasons behind why I was a rag doll, we tried to move on as a happy family, as if nothing had happened. But I felt as if I was a burden to them. Hell, I was a burden to my own self.

After a while I noticed that others looked at me a little differently when I ate. I felt awkward when I ate around people due to what they might possibly be thinking in their head.

"Oh thank God, she's eating. I just hope she doesn't go puke this up. Is that on her nutrition plan? Is she overeating? Is she in control? Look at her eat, I wonder if she fears food."

I felt like a crazy patient in a mental hospital. People were watching my movements to make sure I was not harming myself. Granted, I needed the support but it made me feel angry and paranoid. I started to anticipate my next mishap.

When's it going to be, what's going to set me off next time? Oh, I can't wait! It's going to happen! Oh man!

That is how pathetic I felt.

My mother took me to our physician shortly after my announcement to ask her what they could do to help me. I sat there in the office crying, with my head hanging low. I couldn't even speak for myself. I couldn't even look at the doctor. So my mother began to explain to her about my issue, that I just opened up about being bulimic. She told the doctor that I was not myself, I was sad, that she wanted me to get better and she didn't know what to do for me.

"Therapists, psychiatrists, what do we do?"

I was embarrassed, ashamed, depressed, and most importantly I was hurting myself. Oh how I hated it all, the feeling of being so weak underneath something so evil within me.

The doctor sent me on my way to get blood work done to see how my hormones, my thyroid, and the other enzymes were doing.

Just how badly did you damage yourself, Ella?

The test results showed that my body had stopped producing enough Vitamin D for my body, which explained all of the stress fractures. My thyroid was low, I had low B-complex, and there was hardly any estrogen being produced in my body. All of these things can cause you to feel fatigued and sad.

More medicine for Ella, look at me, I struggle.

The amount of support and empathy that I received was interesting, but what was even more interesting was the amount of messages I received containing sheer ignorance towards eating disorders in general.

Some people said to me "It's just food. Can't you just like stop eating?" People who knew me well looked at me and said "But you're so happy and positive all the time, I don't understand?" Yeah man, me neither!

Others would tell me "You have so much to be happy about, why are you all sad? You've got so much going for you and you do all these insanely hard events, how can you be hindered by food? I don't get it."

Yeah, if it was that simple and easy for me, do you think I'd have had a fork down my throat? Do you think I'd have eaten until I was sick? No it's not like that. It's not the food I'm addicted to it's this demon inside my head. It's complicated, it's misunderstood and I don't expect you to understand it at all because I don't even understand it myself. But I do respect it.

God that shit hurt me to deal with and boy was it annoying. I didn't know how to respond most of the time so I found myself in tears trying to hold back screaming.

"Shit man, I'm just really, really messed up, there's just more to it than that..."

"But Ella, happiness is a choice, stop being sad."

DAMNIT YOU DON'T GET IT! DO YOU REALLY THINK I WANT TO FEEL LIKE THIS EVERYDAY?

Eventually, I ostracized myself from the majority of the people I knew and my circle of friends became even smaller, it almost seemed to shrink by the hour.

Being alone is easy, you don't have to tend to anyone's demands and to their feelings. You have all the time in the world to focus on yourself; or in my case, I had all the time in the world to be lost from myself.

I was also surprised by the lack of hatred towards my eating disorder announcement. Perhaps I was anticipating more judgment than I faced. Although, unfortunately, I did discover shortly after opening up that some individuals I once knew well had judged me.

Some even commented "You look fat and not like an athlete." "Your bulimia issue is weird." "It's embarrassing." "It's insulting." "We don't get it." "Where is your perfection?"

Some of these words end up breaking my heart and I found myself edging more into the darkness as my life unfolded one dirty little truth at a time.

Someone, please, cover me in dirt, that is where true beauty lies, that is the truth.

If I could have just gone ahead and decayed, like the dead bones which rot underneath the free flowing flesh of a lifeless creature lost in the forest, I would have done so already. But it was not my time to rot, it was my time to grow.

I left those 'friends' in the rear view mirror and moved on with my life. Days turned into weeks and weeks turned into months as I slowly mended my way back to a happier Ella. I progressed my way back into a good routine and returned to the reality that I needed to get my life together.

You know, the thing about life is, at least from what I have come to see it as, is that we have all that we really need already and there's no need to search for more.

We already have all that we will ever need in our hands. We have the power to change, the courage to try, the strength to reach out and give. And so in our hands we hold our very own lives. Sometimes our grip strength on our life varies with our knowledge and even without knowing it we go from overloading our life with too much grip to barely holding onto it as it dangles away in the breeze.

Somewhere out there is a way to live with a beautiful balance between crushing life and letting go, and I had lost the notion of what that felt like years before even sticking a fork down my throat became my normality.

My life was in my hands, and as I looked down at them, I saw all that was there; my happiness, my strength, my burritos. It was all in my hands and so I began to pick myself back up. I began to try to eat better. I began to try to grasp my emotions more.

I was better than those who had labelled me. I was wiser than my problems, I was stronger than any ache I had faced.

With the confidence in believing in myself I started to rebuild myself yet again.

Remember, just because people say things about you doesn't mean they're true.

Remember, just because you feel alone doesn't mean you are or have to be.

Like I said before, becoming healthy was a weird feeling for me and it was hard to get rid of the habits that controlled me. The habits that seemed to rage around my races, family events, and the kitchen at my home. They were hard to avoid, hard to move on past, and hard to change because everything was a permeant reminder for me.

Hey, hey, hey, hey Ella, you're weak here.

My father: "Are you healthy?"

Me: "Yeah, I'm good."

My friends: "How are you doing nowadays? You okay?"

Me: "Bad days come and go just like the good, but I am healthy though!"

My sister: "You know you can always talk to me. You are eating right?"

Me: "I always make sure to eat and I know I can. Thanks."

My nutritionist: "Don't let this derail you Ella. How are you mentally?"

Me: "I am okay, much better. I haven't gone off of my nutrition guidelines."

My heart: "Are you doing everything you can do to help yourself?"

Me: "Shhhh... Of course I am. You're silly."

Lies. All of them. They were lies. I was full of them and I couldn't seem to help it.

I continued to lie for a while in attempts to cover up my slip ups, my mistakes, and my dirty habits. I really tried to get healthy but it just felt impossible to me.

It feels as if it is forever in my system to do this, I want it, I hate it, I need it, I despise it. It's confusing as heck.

Ultimately, 'it' is me and it cannot leave me, but I can change it to help better me.

BE GRATEFUL FOR WHAT YOU GOT... IT'S SOMEONE ELSE'S DREAM...

CHAPTER 5
SUCCESS

Designing a masterpiece.

Sculpted from shades of black and white.

Create something full of color from nothing but ashes.

Success is what developed me.

Success is what broke me.

Do not let yourself be defined by anyone other than yourself.

Go out there and make a name that no one will forget.

Be still. Be quiet. This is your moment. I couldn't help but make it out to be more than it was. I couldn't help but feel the jitteriness radiate into my fingers, the anxiety pulsing throughout my body. This was my moment and I brought my awareness to my aches as I bit my lip.

Be still.

Be quiet.

Be ready.

FLAWS DO NOT DEFINE YOU.

I remember that first time toeing the line back in December of 2011. It was cold and raining, just exactly how my mind made it out to be. Everything leading up to the start of the race felt dramatic. Even the droplets of rain falling onto my body seemed to bounce off my skin in an extreme manner.

I got inside my head so much that I began to pace around like a bull. The tension inside me was raging and I was ready to explode.

Let me go, let me go!

Demons were brewing.

Inside my head I kept repeating the vision of finishing the race with my lungs completely taxed, my screams echoing throughout the crowd as I crossed the line first.

My dreams. They was so damn beautiful.

Pacing in bigger circles, I could see in my mind that I was already the champion. I had already won and all the other females and even the males there didn't stand a chance.

I am here now and I am ready.

I was aggressively aching for what awaited me. It hurt.

This is like terrible foreplay, can we just do it already?

At that time of pacing around at the start line in the rain, I had absolutely no idea that this was the race that would get me noticed. I had no idea of the impact it would have on me from that moment.

That moment would change my life in more ways than one.

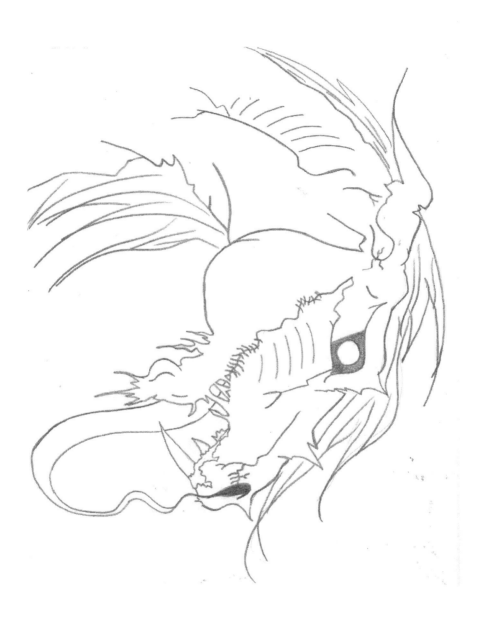

The night before the race, I was filled with all kinds of jitteriness. I had just finished puking up my dinner, the dinner I hardly ate, and I stood there in front of the mirror looking back at my small frame. I watched the ripples of my abdominal muscles slowly move in and out with each breath I took.

This was my obsession and I loved every ounce of it. My music vibrated loudly out of my cell phone as I grasped the bobby pins with my lips and drool began to slide down my chin from concentration. Throwing up my hair into a wicked mohawk, I looked back at myself.

I'm going to win, I'm going to win.

The thought trickled throughout every crevasse in my brain. It was all I could think of.

Greatness.

That night, I did not sleep but for maybe one or two hours. I was restless but I was also a dreamer of all things and my imagination ran vividly. I dreamed of success just like I had been dreaming every night for the past two years. I dreamed of winning and making a name for myself by finally overcoming what seemed to be the ultimate test. The test that held me back from becoming the individual I had always wanted to be.

That was the race where people began to question how to say my last name correctly. It was the race where people actually began to ask who I was, and cheer me on from the sidelines. That was the moment that made me.

I was a blurry image running through the thick rain, yet, I had the still image of what work should look like. I had so much passion flowing through me that I could recall it hurting inside my own joints.

That was the race that started my career and my life.

You ever just feel yourself looking really creepy and also find yourself liking it? Right there in that moment I did and I loved every ounce of it.

Fear Me.

At that start line that early morning I looked over at the other athletes, with my head slightly tilted to the side, my teeth grinding down into each other so hard that my skinny face showed the muscle striations in my jawline. My heavy black makeup streamed down my face as my piercing green eyes glared back at everyone's glimpse.

Slight smirks here and there. I popped my neck and fingers and shook my legs out.

I got this.

I was simply informing everyone in the arena with my body language that I was here to do work and that I wanted to be feared in the best way possible.

"We are Spartans."

The smoke snaked its way through the air, my eyes shifted through the fog, my ears itched for the release... And just like that, we were off. I sprinted towards the pond, my eyes straining to see through the rain that was digging its way into my eyes like needles. Adrenaline pumped through my veins as I scaled the walls and carried the bucket full of sand up the mountain.

I chased down every single man I saw in my sight and yes, I said man because not once did I see a single female on the course as I zipped across the balance beams, crawled through the barbwire, and jumped over the hay bales.

For the first time in a long time, I felt peaceful.

You're such a cliché but you're so good for me. That undeniable grit to compete in such bitter conditions electrified everything and I found the moment to be delicious. The temperature stayed around forty degrees that day and the rain never let up. It was cold, wet and, of course, muddy.

My tights were weighed down with water and mud as they stuck to my quadriceps and with each lengthy stride that stretched forward, my deltoids seemed to pop out of their sockets. My scrawny body lunged forward towards the finish line.

I was about to start something great and I didn't even know it.

That morning I finished first. I screamed my way across the finish line in such joy that I couldn't seem to stop moving after the timing mat.

Everything was just like I had envisioned it. It became a memory that could be put on constant replay and one that will never get old. It sparks a smile each time it cycles through my head.

As I paced around in circles with my hands on the back of my head, with spit running down my chin, and the exhaustion settling into my legs and arms I finally saw all the eyes around me. There were people smiling and clapping for me. I saw their lips mouth "wow", and suddenly, time stopped for a split second. I had done it, I had overcome the biggest obstacle in my life thus far. I had become an athlete.

After that day, the eyes seemed to lock down onto my shaved head and from that point on, my life lost the simplicity of being an unknown.

Prior to running and winning my first ever Spartan Race in December 2011, I had competed in several 5k's, a half marathon, and in my first ever obstacle race which was actually the Tough Mudder event early in the fall of 2011.

It was in that Tough Mudder where I stumbled into the world of mud running and all it took was an article in a fitness magazine saying "try a Tough Mudder, marathons are boring". Immediately I thought to myself "Holy shit that's right, I'm freaking bored out of my mind."

I was intrigued with the ropes, the mud, the heavy objects, and the walls to climb so I registered for it on that very day without any hesitation.

All I needed was a chance to believe in myself and I jumped at its first showing.

I quickly made my way to becoming one of the top athletes to hit the obstacle and endurance racing circuit. It was all beyond weird to me. I was hugging strangers just about everywhere I went, taking photos with googley eyed fans.

I finished on the podiums with every race I competed in. Companies were sending me offers left and right, and magazines were emailing me for interviews.

It all seemed like a fairy tale, a dream come true, and the best part about it all was the secrets I hid from everyone including my own self. It really looked like I had my shit together but don't let me fool you, I was one tricky son of a biscuit because I was doing so well yet struggling so hard.

From 2011 to 2014, I competed in many grueling events that ranged anywhere from a Death Race (which is known for its 10-15% completion rate and can last up to 90 hours) to a GORUCK or a Spartan Race (distances vary from five to fourteen miles while doing military style obstacles throughout). I even competed in one bodybuilding competition, various long distance horse races, and many other events that lasted anywhere from a few minutes to a few days.

My face was out there in the world of extreme sports, performing at the top of the game, all while dealing with several physical and mental issues. As I slaved through my own self-induced labors, I was asked by many "How do you keep going after all you have gone through?"

It's simple really; let me ask you, what do you do during the winter when you find yourself feeling cold? You put on a jacket to get the warmth you so desire and need. Now let's say that jacket doesn't do you justice, so you grab more winter items to help you stay warm, you put on a beanie, a scarf, or perhaps another jacket. You do what you need to and then some to stay warm and to avoid the cold.

That's simply all I was doing. I was doing what I needed to do, and then some, to function properly.

The light is warm, obviously.

I would finally come to terms with the fact that relapsing is part of my recovery and a part of coming to terms with my disorder, but it is without a doubt the most frustrating feeling to find yourself in.

I went through phases from March to May 2014 where I was semi clean from my sins and found my dirty habits came forth only around races or shows.

Just when it finally seemed that I had got a grip of my eating disorder, the Summer Death Race rolled around in June and I became dark again.

Never mind my lack of addiction and sober life, free from my binge eating. The week before the race I became completely numb again which caused me to stop training and begin to eat. I ate and I ate, unhealthy amounts of food leading up to the event.

There goes my hard work, again.

I sure do hate this repetition of 'again.'

The Death Race in 2014 was only a few days after my twenty first birthday and I made my way up to Vermont feeling pretty decent about my life (more like *trying* to feel that way). But I was not all that bright inside, this disorder ruined my competitions.

I made my way up North to the gorgeous mountains wherein lurked so many of my nightmares and dreams. I was ready to suffer. This year I was hoping for a skull.

The binging prior to this event had caused me to be a bit heavier than I'd hoped for but I tried to block out my gut's pain and think positively, I could do this.

The race began on Friday morning and I ended up competing extremely well, conquering tedious tasks of making fire, orienteering, sewing my own buckskin outfit and covering about hundred miles until hour thirty-nine where I got disqualified due to a technicality.

The task was quiet simple, you must complete a thirty six matching test covering ancient explorers in history, the only way you can move on from this task is if you get all the answers correct and any answer that is incorrect results in you being disqualified from the event itself.

The twist on it is you cannot talk or even really look at any other competitor. You can only ask Jack, one of the race directors, one yes or no question at a time but before doing so you must hold a yoga pose for either ten or twenty minutes then stand in line, wait, ask your question and then go back to do another yoga pose.

I did this for seven and a half hours until finally my mind relaxed too much and an auto response reaction screwed me over.

It was almost midnight and I was hunched over in an awkward back yoga pose. My body was beginning to feel a little cold, but for the most part I was content. Athletes had been dropping left and right. Some were quitting due to frustration and most were accidentally being caught talking so they were pulled from the race. As I laid there in the dark with my ankles next to my ears, I drifted into a light sleep... "259, 259, get in line!" the girl said out loud to me and in my sleeping slumber, I regretfully responded without even acknowledging it. "Okay."

As soon as the words left my lips, my heart dropped. It ripped open and out came my emotions. "Oh god what have I done?" I put my hands on my face, I couldn't tell if this was real yet. But rest assured I heard her quietly say to me "Ella... I have to pull you from the race. Everyone behind me heard you. I'm so sorry, I don't want to do this but I have to."

Still in huge disbelief, I sat up and as I did, I began to scream and burst into tears "I wanted to finish, my body is good, I wanted to finish, my body is good!"

My heart broke and I sat there sobbing amongst the remaining athletes as two of my friends ran toward me. I was not even exactly sure of who it was at first but they held me as I cried my heart out into their arms. I buried my face into their warm bodies, and grabbed their jackets to pull them into my sorrow. I wanted to believe that it was all just a nightmare so that I could escape my other nightmare: my life.

I wanted to finish so badly and my body was truly there. I wasn't suffering from trench foot or hot blisters, no doubts had crept into my head. I knew that I could do this, I enjoyed every ache and I truly needed its pain, but it was stripped away from me.

I slipped. I fucking slipped!

They took my bib from me and I was dropped from the race just like that. I looked over at my friends standing in line waiting their turn to see Jack and as I approached them I could sense my humble breakdown approaching. I collapsed into their arms while they hugged me tightly, some filled with teary eyes. I looked back at them. "Kill it for me."

Handing over my bib that night felt as if I was handing over my soul to the devil. I didn't want to do it. My head hung low like a coward's does when he gets caught with some dumb brunette from the bar and apologizes to his wife. Agh the shame was so vibrant. I wanted to be blind. Was this really happening?

I'm silly. I slipped up. How could I?

I WANTED THIS SO BADLY.

I stumbled my way up to the top of the summit where all of the other DNF bibs lay. Embarrassment, shame, and regret seemed to sizzle through my veins as I dropped my bib down onto the ground. I quickly turned around, sniffling up my tears. I needed to get away from there.

I was stubborn and ended up rucking three miles back to Amee Farm where my crew member, and one of my best friends and easily one of the greatest people I know of in this world, Patrick, came running up to greet me. There was nothing really to be said to each other and so we just hugged. I cried into his arms for a few minutes.

"Come on cheetah girl. Let's go."

We made our way back down to base camp where he bundled me up in some blankets and I fell asleep crying in a chair. I was awoken the next morning by some friends back at the cabin house and I was immediately confused as to why I was in a bed. Then I came to the harsh realization.

I'm not competing anymore, I got disqualified.

I hated the fact that I was in a bed.

This isn't where I should be.

I hate it.

I finally had my first real meal that morning which consisted of pancakes, bacon, and eggs. Yes it was amazing, but I felt guilty about it; guilty for being out of the race and for eating.

The thought "I don't deserve this meal" sank into my head.

Shit here we go.

I returned to the race site to help crew for the rest of the competitors out there who were still looking at another twenty something hours left of competing.

During my time competing, I traveled alongside one of my best friends, Mark Webb, who has been one of the biggest influences and supporters on curing myself.

We covered the majority of that event together up and down those mountains, sharing dumb sexual jokes, enjoying pure moments of silence, and talking about life as we did 1500 'burpees', but they were more like 'bitch burpees'.

That morning as I arrived to help the other athletes, I saw him still out there competing, I ran into his arms and we cried into each other's arms for a brief moment, "I should still be right next to you Webb, but I'm proud of you."

I was filled with an overwhelming sense of pride and it strained my heart as I wrapped up other's feet, handed them food, and rubbed their shoulders. I wanted to be them.

It did, however, feel nice to be able to help so many others out but I also hated that I was not out there with them suffering.

For the rest of the trip I assisted others to achieve their well-deserved skulls.

Sulking into my disappointment some, I returned home to Texas a bit overwhelmed about what exactly had happened and how I could have let myself slip like that.

But to be honest, I got over it pretty well and it was not the fact that I failed in the race that necessarily caused me to become so depressed again, it was just my routine, the usual for me. It was what I'd been doing for years. It was ingrained in my head that this was my religion and it was time for me to give up some money.

I went numb after every race but that Death Race especially broke me down and I ended up severely relapsing after it.

Back to that lifestyle I hated. Back to the Ella that I didn't even know, and back into the familiar sadness that caused me to avoid people even if they were friends and family.

I ate so much again that I could not fit into my clothes. I was embarrassed about my physique, confused, scared, and it felt like this was REALLY never going to end for me. I was so sick of being sick.

The next few months after the Death Race were pieces of shit. I was stuck back into a constant sickening, confusing, controlling, depressing, painful, cycle of relapsing with my eating disorder. I started to pack on weight and ate all the things, all the time.

My once finely sculpted hardbody got soft AGAIN and I grew heavy. My fine lines were now gone, the hardness of my muscles disappeared, and all of my clothes were now tight around my legs, butt, stomach, and chest.

Sigh. I am expanding again.

There went my mind and that time everything seemed more painful because of the fact that I was so familiar with the pain. It just sickened me to the core and not long into my suffering I weakened. It was too much for me and I considered giving up.

I contemplated my choices in life. Perhaps I was not cut out to be an athlete. Perhaps I should really just give up on this genius idea of doing all of these crazy events already. My body and my mind couldn't seem to tolerate it.

I am pathetic, I am pitiful.... I am... I am lost in my relapse.

It's the relapsing of my behaviors alone that seems to hurt me the most.

I often get asked "How do you do such intense events? How do you compete for days, going off of very little sleep, hardly any food, your body is destroyed, how and why do you do it?"

Because I'm crazy.

Because I simply just like it.

Because I get quiet in the head.

Because I'm really good at numbing out pain.

There's many reasons as to why I do such crazy intense events, mainly because I've lived in such great pain that I can find comfort while self-inducing it upon myself.

Sometimes you'll find me literally out in the woods for days, living out of a rucksack, carrying objects that should be too heavy for me to carry, but I do it and, most importantly, I enjoy it. Mainly because my head actually gets quiet, I can forget my demons, I'll lose the pressure on my shoulders and replace it with a log. I don't even acknowledge my fame anymore, because at times of pure agony, I am just me.

But as to how, it's really just a matter of doing what you need to do and then some. I turn a part of my brain off and turn another part on. I forget my emotions, my conscious and I function off terms of survival.

I'll continue to preach this way of thinking in regards to competing until the day I die, I do what I need to get it done and then some.

The end of the summer and fall of 2014 went as follows:

Binge for a day, be clean for four days, binge for three days, clean for two days, binge for two days, be clean for four days, binge for three days, binge for two days, be clean for one day, binge for three days, be clean for two days, binge for a day, be clean for a day, binge for a day, be clean for four days, binge for two days, be clean for six days, binge for one day, be clean for three days, binge for two days, be clean for seven days, binge for three days, be clean for two days, binge for three days, be clean for a day, binge for a day, be clean for nine days, binge for two days, be clean for four days, binge for three days, be clean for seven days, binge for two, etc.

Life went on as a constant battle hour by hour, day by day. I couldn't even keep any promises, not even to myself. I had to tell myself what I was good at, to remember that I don't quit on myself.

So don't quit now but man!

Letting go of 'letting go' is real hard.

I got so tired of all of the emotional stress. That alone was enough to keep me going, away from those behaviors and to start to implement tactics to help stop the binging and to help save my own life.

I decided to try to find more healthy distractions, and with the guidance of a therapist, I began to get back on my horse in the evenings. I took five minute meditations anytime I felt the pressure to eat out of control. I drank glasses of water before and after meals. I went for walks, I wrote, I sketched my demonic ponies. I did what I needed to do and then some so I could move on and find the peace that I desired so badly.

Getting back onto my nutrition plan seemed to be an impossible task for me. The constant failing kept making me believe that I was never going to change my situation, so I'd just eat and cry because that's all I was good at those days anyway.

My once relaxed and flexible approach to my everyday diet transformed into a huge annoying stressor for me. I became fixated on logging all of my food into an app on my iPhone, counting the macros down to the gram, and weighing my food for every meal.

It seemed to make me lose my mind even more. Instantly overwhelmed, I freaked out about the stress and sought out a cave to crawl into. I just wanted to be alone. I also stopped trying to follow my diet plans.

Forgetting how to just eat and fuel my body made the feeling of being a fool soak deep down into my heart, and no matter how much I tried to think otherwise or do differently, it was in my blood that I had to depend on devices or plans to know how to eat. It was like I was this weak newborn waiting to suck on my mother's breasts.

This was the only way I lived, by depending on my world when my world had already ruined me.

Anything that dealt with food stressed me out and so I started to shut people out again. I wanted to be alone. It was easy for me, but nothing is ever *that* easy for me.

Depression is a selfish coward, he wants all of you, he doesn't care what you want or what's best for you. He decides what happens and what you want. He wanted me to be alone, so the easiest thing for me to do with depression's guidance was to shut out my world, to go numb.

Not long into my counseling I was put on anti-depressants as an aide to help my mood and get my sadness in control. It was such an odd experience for me to have.

I'm someone who is known for having such strength but on that day, I looked over at my doctor and cried to her, repeating the same thing over and over.

"I'm just so sad. I want it to go away. I'm not Ella. I want it to go away."

My hands trembled as I hugged my torso, feeling the softness of my stomach pressing against my forearms, a deep pressure in my chest. I couldn't breathe properly; my eyes were burning with tears; the salvia in my mouth tasted like metal.

She looked at me, her soft blue eyes shining with hope, reassuring me. "You're doing so much for yourself. You're doing all that you can. You're getting help and that's more than many do."

A moment of silence fell between the two of us as I wiped away my tears.

"So what's next?"

She looked over at me calmly and began to explain to me that she was going to first start me on a mild dosage of anti-depressants. She glanced over at her laptop, back at me, then back at the computer. I knew it had been coming, my therapist suggested it, my friends suggested it, even my own head did and now it was really happening.

My doctor was talking to me about different kinds of anti-depressants but my head was spinning. I could hardly listen to her as she went over the side effects of them and when she finished explaining it all to me, she looked back over at me.

"How does this make you feel?"

I hate that question. Like what, really, how does being on some medication just so I can find a smile make me feel? If I'm going to be blunt here, I freaking hate that.

I didn't really know how to feel at that moment, so for a split moment I fumbled with my words.

I wanted to be better so badly but I also disliked the thought that I needed a substance to get me there, that I couldn't actually pull this through on my own. The fact that I had to be dependent on medicine to help bring me some sort of peace hit my pride.

Bite your lip; swallow.

My face was dumbfounded as I told her that I wanted them.

It took me three years to realize that during all that time I didn't know who I actually was. I was trying so hard to be something great that I couldn't even look in the mirror and see how much I had already done with my life already, that I was and that I am great, always.

It was a hard pill to swallow but I bit my lip and masked over my fresh wounds, let go of my pride and attended my therapy every Wednesday morning for a couple of months. I shriveled up inside as I looked over at my doctor as she sat delicately in her chair, her face was so calm and loving as she listened to me sob. I was so tired of the pain and the confusion. I was just so sad all the time.

"I really do want to be healthy, I want to change my life, I want to reach my potential and it's me holding me back, help me."

Being sick is easy. It's easy to be extreme with your life because all you really have to do is let go of a lot of things and just say 'fuck it' as you destroy something beautiful like it's nothing. You let go of all hope for this fatal attraction you have because it hits you like ecstasy and makes you go numb. The world doesn't exist in that moment, and you are free to destroy and create. But guess what, you'll never feel that high again.

Being healthy is hard for me to become. It's a hard balance between the knowledge of having a heavy heart and what letting go is like to reminiscing about a time when your heart was never heavy and you were crushing life. Somewhere out there is a neutral area between the two and I will find this with guidance.

Going to therapy did help me, even if it was just in very microscopic ways at first but once I actually said my problems out loud to someone and discussed ways to change it, I eventually started to notice small changes within me.

For example, instead of letting a small mishap or something go off in my day, I started taking five minutes to mediate, to think, would eating all this yogurt and all this bread benefit me?

Think of all the hard work you've been doing, Ella, is it worth it? It never is.

It was never worth it to stuff my face with a tremendous amount of food, hesitate about forcefully puking it up, and then repeating it for the next few hours which ended up becoming a couple of days.

It's not worth it, you're better than that.

ALL THINGS ELLA

The old Ella:

Just waking up and hearing my demons: feel numb and go binge.

Eat a big meal and feel full: feel guilty and go binge.

Have some dessert with my family: feel ashamed and go binge.

Go to a friend's and eat something not on my meal plan: feel numb and go binge.

Attend a party and resist food: feel frustrated and go binge.

Attend a party and eat food freely: feel ashamed and go binge.

Get into an argument with the parents: feel angry and go binge.

Debit card gets denied: get frustrated and go binge.

Wake up later than desired: feel lazy and go binge.

You're out of egg whites: feel frustrated and go binge.

An old friend texts and asks to hangout: get anxious and go binge.

These habits still live inside me, occasionally I can forget them and act without letting my eating disorder control me, however, other times it wins.

There's always ways to simplify your fight. I have learned ways to try to prevent them like putting sticky notes in my special peanut butter cabinet.

Think of your hard work, is it worth it?

I make sure to eat in different places than my kitchen, and if I do eat in my kitchen, I make sure to drink a big glass of water and leave as soon as I'm done with my meal.

I began to talk to strangers openly about my issues without getting emotional and not long after graduating massage school I got a half sleeve tattoo that resembled my battles with my eating disorder.

I found myself proud of my fight.

I'll babble to strangers about the ink on my right arm, explaining to them with an overwhelming sense of accomplishment. The grin on my face is one a fool would own. My voice gets loud as I tell them.

"The woman on my arm resembles me in a way but she is also someone else, she is the goddess of temptation and in one of her arms she holds an apple that has a bite taken out of it. An apple resembles knowledge and it's also food, I was very aware of how damaging an eating disorder could be, but the goddess of temptation inside me was too hungry and so I went ahead and took a bite out of it. In her other hand she holds a chain that wraps around to the inner of my bicep, the chain connects to a leopard which resembles my future. Never in my life would I have suspected I would be known as a cheetah or a leopard; a creature so fierce."

I made it seem like it was a bit easy, easy to change such abusive behaviors, it wasn't and it isn't. Change occurred slowly within me. Technically, it wasn't the food that was ruining my life, it was my behaviors and to adjust those will take lots time.

Embrace it, endure it, and you will overcome it.

While writing this book, I debated about doing this section. I didn't know how to go about it, but I knew the importance of finding my old writings and sorting them together properly to create this section because it would do wonders.

I want to destroy your minds, in a positive way for I've come such a long way in many ways.

After doing so and reading where I was back then, I am extremely glad I did due to the fact that I have continued to grow in so many ways. It was a very hard process to go back and relive some of those moments but they are here and they will forever be a part of me, although they do not define me anymore.

The following are snip bits from my personal journals that I have kept since the time of my accident to when I began training. I wrote everything down, including my wicked thoughts, workout splits, everything that I consumed, and everything that consumed me.

Enjoy my construction.

These first journal entries are from the year 2007, pre and post back surgery. The exact days are not recorded very well but my pain was. I was thirteen at the time of these writings.

Entry 1:

I cannot sleep because of the pain. It's 1:12 a.m. They just don't know how much pain I'm in. This is so hard, the pain is unbearable and I'm trying not to show it and suck it up. I can't believe this happened to me.

It all started about two years ago and I've been struggling to cope with it since. It feels like someone stabbing my spine and they are poking and jabbing me.

My smiles are gone.

I've thrown up twice and fainted twice.

I can't stand this throbbing, stabbing, pain. Right side

Entry 2:

Mom doesn't know my pain, neither does my dad. "Be Tough" is my dad's words.

I had to wear a hard brace for six weeks. I wore it for two. It was extremely uncomfortable and painful. I was very emotional about it. I hated it. Want to burn it.

Entry 3:

Physical therapy is making me very uncomfortable. I threw up today, the pain is that bad. I can barely walk and I am just crying too much. I want it to go away.

I threw up because of physical therapy, I don't like him at all.

Entry 4:

The doctor said surgery is the only option now and if I'm in this much pain I need to do it and not do physical therapy, I understand.

Stabbing pain now.

Continuously, it never ends.

It's the first time I have truly prayed for God and for him to take me out.

Entry 5:

Surgery.

Surgery.

Surgery.

Surgery.

Last thing left. I'm in so much pain.

I'm scared, it hurts. I could get paralyzed.

It hurts so bad, I'm going through hell.

Entry 6:

Today is Thursday, January 25th. Yesterday we went to Dr. Williams at Children's Hospital (a big place!) and had some x-rays done. My discs have slipped forward out of my spine. So, he told us that this will never heal and that I had to have surgery. But there's got to be more he says, if we don't go in and do exploratory surgery, I could be crippled. So we scheduled my surgery for: February 19th, 2007.

At seven or nine in the morning, hopefully seven I have to go donate blood for my own self, because a lot of my blood will go away during my surgery.

Needles: Terrified, petrified, faint?

Entry 7:

I can't remember the last time I truly laughed or smiled. Truly. I'm in so much pain that I can't control. My emotions, I sit with no words, every day is a challenge for me. Everyday normal stuff like going down or upstairs, it's like climbing a mountain. Going to the restroom, I need help getting out of the bathtub, sleeping.... I haven't slept good in a long time. Walking and sitting are extremely painful.

The way I'm trying to deal with the pain is to be quiet and cry. But now I am too weak to cry, too weak to stand and too weak for school. And now I'm really quiet.

It's hard to go to school and focus and ignore the stabbing, sharp pain.

I can't wait for the pain to be gone.

Entry 8:

Friday 26th, 2007.

Blood donation at 2:30pm, I didn't faint, unbelievable! (maybe for a second).

It was so scary, I was shaking. It took about twenty minutes to draw the blood and it hurt. My arm is going to be sore for a couple days. They also pricked my finger and it didn't really bleed so she kept squeezing my finger. it wasn't cool.

Entry 9:

It's the 27th now.

I feel sick. Achy sharp: 9-10.

The new medicine doesn't work at all anymore. I'm in so much pain that my face was flooded with tears and I threw up. I feel so light headed and sick from the pain, it's controlling me.

Entry 10:

Eighteen days until my (scary) surgery.

Yesterday, we had an assembly in school and I sat up at the top of the bleachers with my pillow but my back was hurting so bad. I tapped Mrs. Smith's shoulder and whispered in her ear, "I feel sick, my back hurts". And then I choked up in tears as we slowly got me out of the bleachers, I could barely walk.

"Let it rip." She said.

And I sobbed. I limped with pain I can barely describe but only one word can give some insight, hell. It felt like murdering hell.

She got me to Mrs. Mumm and I laid down, we put the heating pack on my back and I squeezed the longhorn thing she had. My mom came and got me and I came home.

Today was a bad day.

Entry 11:

I seriously want the pain to go away, I can't stand this anymore.

It's stabbing me like pain, then throbbing like a heart, it's a headache like dizziness.

It's only February 3rd.

I can't.

Entry 12:

Sunday, February 4th. I threw up twice today, ten and seven this morning. The pain is horrible and last night I couldn't keep feeling like I was going to throw up. So today, Monday, I'm home and I feel so bad. My back is so sharp.

Entry 13:

February 7th, today is Casey's birthday.

I am extremely weak and in so much pain. I can't stand it, it's hard and getting harder for me to cope with. It's easy to cry, I feel so light headed, dizzy, and like I'm going to throw up every second. My back is such a weird feeling. I don't know how to describe it. It's hurting real bad right now, my surgery is in twelve days and it seems like too long of a wait.

Entry 14:

February 9th, ten days.

I'm staying home today, I feel sick. My back feels weird, I really just don't know how to explain the pain. It's so sharp. My eyes are so swollen from crying and my entire body is extremely weak. Yesterday Haylee had to help me to my car, I was crying and in a lot of pain.

I got another get well present from Aunt Linda. It was a Trail of Painted Ponies statue she bought me the: Blue Medicine one. and a small indian one It's beautiful, I love it. I'm going to bring the small indian one to the hospital. It will make me smile.

Entry 15:

February 11th, eight more days.

My back is extremely sensitive and in a lot of stabbing pain from the sides of my body. I feel horrible, I'm sore.

Tuesday: pre-surgery visit at 11:30am but Mom and Dad just go.

Friday the 16th, I have more blood work.

I packed my things I want to bring to the hospital.

Entry 16:

February 14th, it's valentine's day. I got lots of candy.

Tomorrow is my last day of school. I'm not feeling good and I'm really nervous and my back is really hurting.

I will look half-dead like.

Tubes coming out of me.

Major surgery.

I'm going to do good.

I'm tired.

Four or five hours long, oh boy. But it'll seem like four or five minutes for me, I think. I don't know what to expect!

I want a laptop for my story. Wireless. With internet. I'm going to publish my book.

Entry 17:

Mrs. Townes really knows how much pain I'm in and knows what I am going through. She seems to be the only one that knows. My last day of school, she hugged me and kissed me on the head and told me "you'll do fine and I'll come see you Tuesday."

Entry 18:

I love to ride. I can't ride. I will ride again because I love it. I'm going to do it again, just you wait.

Entry 19:

There's no way to describe correctly how much pain I am in. It's so horrible, it's murder. First it's soreness and achy, then stabbing pain that goes down my entire back and butt- psh, my butt is so sore. Then the stabbing pain shoots down and throbs into a heart. Makes me extremely weak, it hurts me so greatly. I can take a bullet now.

Entry 20:

If someone says they have a high pain tolerance of pain, how about they try this:

A very sharp pain that stabs your spine, tickles down with needles and pauses down into your butt and throbs like a heartbeat. Leaving aches to vibrate throughout the remainder of your body.

Entry 21:

It's the 18th.

Well today is my last day, I'm going to go play with Mimosa and all the other horses. I took a look at my english saddle. It's so dusty, it made my eyes water. I miss riding. I wish I could be racing Socks right now, Riding with that strong bond we have, I feel guilty she gets no time under the saddle anymore.

Grandma and grandpa came home late last night. Grandma looks good for her age and grandpa, well he's just so special.

Why did this happen to me?

Entry 22:

Socks, you helped me laugh, you dried my tears and because of you I have no fears. Together we live, together we grow, teaching each other what we must know. You came in my life and I was blessed, I love you, you are the best, I have to release my hands and say goodbye for now, please my friend, don't you cry. I promise you this, it's not the end. Cause like I said, you're my best friend.

Entry 23:

18th, last day!

It's 9pm, the night before surgery, I'm nervous but it is a different kind of nervous. A sick like feeling in my gut. Tomorrow is the big day and I get to choose what smell I use to make me sleep, I wonder what flavors they have.

I laid out my clothes, we have to get up at 4:30am to get there on time. My back is fully packed and now I need to try to sleep. Good luck.

It's going to be hard to sleep extra tonight. I spent time with the horses, feeding them treats they didn't need. Grandma bought me some shoes, they were vans, some silky pink zebra pajama pants. I'm in good hands.

For some reason, I have a feeling something bad is going to happen..

My friend's said their going to come see me, I hope they do, It'll make me smile. My first surgery and it's a major one.

4:15am. I'm already awake, my body can feel the warmth of my bed. My back is achy.

It's now on the thirty minute mark and I can hear mom coming up the stairs, it's time to go.

Entry 24:

I was so nervous. It was extremely long on waiting for the nurse to call my name. When she finally called 'Ella', my heart raced. She walked us to the room, I didn't want to go really.

They put the bracelets on my wrists and went over my allergies to drugs.

My nurse's name was Miss Kellie. She showed me pictures of the IV's and the gas smells, I choose watermelon, it was a very strong sent. Then the bed came in and some nurses put on my hair mask. As they rolled me through the hallways, the smell of frozen blood and rubber gloves filled the air. My eyes started to water in nervous tears.

"Miss Ella Kociuba comin' in", she cheerfully yelled out as she rolled me into the surgery room. I was so nervous but it all happened so fast. I was getting weaker and more frightened by the second, the room was freezing.

When I was in the surgery room, all the nurses and doctors came by my side, grabbing my arms and legs. They put the sleeping mask onto my face and I began to look around. Seeing stuff I wish I didn't see and then my eyes were so heavy that I went out.

Big lights.

Big machines.

Nurses.

Knives.

They put the mask on me. That strong smell quickly putting me out. My eyes got very heavy and I started to see the darkness.

The thing that I don't get is that why didn't anyone see this? I have had lots of x-rays, MRI's, CT Scans, and bone scans. Why did it take so long?

Entry 25:

Nine hours later it took. They found that my spine was never connected to my tailbone. A birth defect that Dr. Williams had no idea how I could do all that I did what with my spine the way it was, it was amazing to him. He put four metal bolts to connect my back and butt then two big screws to align, fix, secure, and stable my back. My major surgery is over.

Entry 26:

When they awoke me, I moaned and yelled in pain. My dad said I looked like the exorcist girl, I was grabbing, crying, and screaming with my pale face.

I can't remember much but it was so painful that I do know.

I fell asleep several times and awoke only for a few seconds. But without my medicine I could not sleep and even then, it was hard to fall asleep to the aches.

I also didn't eat for two days after my surgery, just slept and took meds.

I had four IV's, they finally took out the three big ones and left the small on in my wrist. I hate needles so much.

Entry 27:

Physical therapy was so extremely painful. Stabbing pain everywhere, I can't even begin to describe how horrible it is.

Making me walk, it's so hard. I miss how simple life once was.

Entry 28:

Smokin' hot temperature. I was burning hot during the five of the days while I was in the hospital, it was miserable, I was miserable.

Entry 28:

On the day I was going to go home, Asher, the hospital dog came to see me. It make me smile! I got lots of balloons and animals.

I can peel the skin off my lips.

It also took me a long time to go to the restroom and walk on my own. My lips got so very chapped and my voice was so scratchy.

Entry 29:

If I were to die, I'd like that this journal be kept forever and my ashes to be spread around with my closest of friends. I don't need to name them, my friends know who they are and what they mean to me. I love everyone, I really do.

Some of the people who said they would come visit me. Well they didn't. That sucked.

I'm weak and my arms are bruised up. My scar is bandaged and it's very, very long.

My car ride home was even longer, it was horrible. Dad seemed to drive crazy but I know he was trying his hardest to be careful. But every little bump, turn, stop, and line on the road caused my back to throb open. I feel so miserable.

It's tearing my heart not being able to ride.

Entry 30:

I couldn't sleep at night at all, the bed is too painful. All of my nurses were very nice to me and I loved them all. But Sarah was the one who pushed me the most and I didn't really like her all that much but I guess it was her job.

Entry 31:

It's Sunday and I feel much stronger but I am still very weak and I am so sore. I went outside today, Coca and Mimosa played in the big pasture. The sun felt so good on my pale skin as I watched the horses run around. Coca herding the pack, he is so silly. The warm sun and light breezes calmed me and the puppies running around chasing the cats made me happy. I squeezed my pig stuffed animal when my back would throb. Later that day I walked to the barn! Maybe the dark circles underneath my eyes will go away.

Entry 32:

I keep getting a heavy feeling in my back and it's making me get very dizzy.

Entry 33:

It felt good to walk but I got tired extremely fast.

"I wanna see Socks."

Socks recognized me immediately and she rubbed her head onto my hands. I fed her cookies.

Entry 34:

12:36am: I can't sleep at all, my back is killing me- so is my stomach.

I feel:

*) Oily face

*) Knotted greasy hair

*) Achy, weak back

*) Extreme back pain

*) Sweaty skin

*) Cramping legs

*) Sharp stomach pain

*) Bruised arms and wrists

Entry 35:

Stronger me, it's Monday. I walked a lot today, to the mail box! Uphill was so tiring, but I did it! I did it! I sat outside for a long time today. Mimosa was galloping in big circles today by herself.

I feel stronger today but still get weak and tired really fast.

Entry 36:

Yesterday Mrs. Townes, Mrs. Smith, and Mrs. Mumm came to visit me, nice. They brought over two big banners with all my classmates signatures and notes were on it. And a card signed by all the teachers.

Entry 37:

My back is very painful today, it's sharp and throbbing crazily. Tired.

Entry 38:

Thursday, the 28th, I went to the see the doctor today and got my dressings changed. I can finally take a shower now! I saw my scar, it's not as long as

I thought it was, but it's still pretty long. It's very touchy and scabby. I had to get more x-rays today to see how the metal is. It hurt so bad to lay down on the hard machine, I was in tears.

I saw the bolts and screws, it looks so freaky. You can even see where the break is and where my birth defect was.

Entry 39:

Friday the 29th.

Today is another bad day again, it's hurting a lot and I want to take a shower but I can't without any help and I need to feel better first. I took a pill not long ago and for some reason I'm really tired, I didn't get much sleep last night at all.

Mrs. Holly just left visiting me, she's my favorite teacher, she helped me figure out that I could write.

Lots of people have been caring for me, which I thank with all my heart, yay!

Entry 40:

Mom is gone and I need her, I'm very tired and in a lot of pain. My back is NOT doing so hot the last few days. Just really uncomfortable.

It almost feels like I'm stretching it out, it's so sharp and walking is so hard to do. I lost some weight, my bots in my back weigh not that much, I don't think.

Entry 41:

Monday the 5th.

Two weeks since my surgery, my right leg hurts when I walk and I'm just in bad shape. It's very hard to walk for a little bit, it's hard but I'm really trying hard.

I just want to ride my horse.

Before decompression I was able to ride and workout with the pain, it still hurt but I could tolerate it, it was very hard to do it but I was in love. Riding horses, I have found what I want to do for the rest of my life.

The last day before I started treatment with the doctor, I worked out a little bit in basketball practice. Coach Hightower never really let me workout all that much cause she knew I was in pain, but I just want to play.

Basketball gets out at 5:30, mom gets me around 6. I come home and quickly change into jeans and slip on a sweater. It's always real dark outside but I don't mind, I like it but I don't like the cold.

I get socks tacked up in the old english leather saddle we have and I put a towel under it to warm her hips. She's so beautiful. She dips her head down for her bridle and I slip her bit into her mouth, but first I warm the cold metal with my hands. Even though it was cold that night, I braided her thick mane.

When I get up on her back, I feel a sharp pull in my back, ignore it, I'm doing what I love. Go away!

We trotted along the road and did the bunny loop several times, as soon as we passed Debbie's house, I urged her into a wild canter. I always feel like we're just one being. We run pass the 'African tree' and smoothly ran the turn up the hill. I kicked Socks to go faster, she exploded up the hill, I yell out "I love you, let's go!" She threw up her head and jumped to the top of the hill, we then trotted the dark curves around the groups of the trees.

It was a fun ride and I miss it, so much, a lot! I miss the smell of horse sweat on leather, the motion of riding and being as one. The bond we have and just the simple smell of a horse is the best.

Entry 42:

It's a Tuesday, cool.

I had a horrible throbbing headache all day and my back was very achy, I guess just surgery pain lingering.

Mornings are the hardest for me and so are late afternoons. I need pills all the time. Going for walks feels good to my head too.

I stay up late watching re-runs of 'Who's Line Is It Anyways? Eating ruffle chips by their ruffles. My back aches as I hold my pig stuffed animal close to my belly, I think it will always hurt me, it always has.

After I get tired of that show I watch Bam's Unholy Union, I think he is really cool even though he's so wild. I wish he wasn't marrying sissy missy.

I sip water slowly so that I don't have to go to the restroom cause that means I'll have to get up and that hurts.

Entry 43:

I WENT UPSTAIRS TODAY!

Really tiring but I did it! Really hard though, I about passed out several times and after it I pretty much was dead. I started to write my story on the computer, I wish I had internet up there.

Mrs. Brownlee is coming to see me today!

I'm getting so much better!

Mrs. Brownlee just left and so did Niki. I even talked to Haylee on the phone for a while, she stayed over for like two years!!! I love her. We laughed and laughed, I'm going to get better, I'll walk up the stairs one day and not have to cry.

Entry 44:

This surgery saved my life and right before it, I could hardly walk. If I hadn't had this surgery I would never be walking again.

I'm now to the point where I'm able to walk by myself, mother stays close by my side, but I'm doing it by myself. Sometimes I have to use the walls, but I'm getting better.

This is the last page of this notebook so I guess I'll talk to you later.

Journal ends and new life begins to unfold as I grow:

December 10th, 2010:

Tonight I've realized and seen how much pain in one can change one's self. How it slowly develops in you, even after it's happened long ago. Chance put up a fight for his blanket. I struggled to show him it was okay. We were out in his paddock when the sudden rush of emotions over took me. I soon began to cry to him. He pinned his ears up and we seemed to look into each other's eyes. "What'd they do to you boy?" I asked. He then walked back into the warmth of his stall filled with hay. I cried in the cold darkness by myself. I didn't really understand why I was crying, I don't quite understand abuse, I will never understand pain. I wish I could keep the ones I love safe and give them what they need. I guess it was my heart cracking and aching tonight at the realization of what other's words and actions can do to someone or something.

I saw his anger from his past showing. It might be the present but what happened yesterday makes today. No one or no thing is created evil it can be made by its surroundings. He has challenged me as a rider, as a human, as a leader, and as an athlete. He's taught me that even the greatest things can come from misfortunes. He's a strong, lonesome horse. He chooses to be alone and refuses what he doesn't want. His mind is twisted with the past and I think I know how he feels.

He is my horse. He is my buddy. And he is my hero.

January 6th, 2010:

It's January and I'm not having much of a life. So I've taken some time to notice some things. I've seen that nothing ever, technically, goes to plan. One or more things go differently than you imagined it for the fifth time. So, what's the point of even planning something out? Why don't we just let everything fall as it would without our attempts at guiding it? You know? Some of the greatest things ever came from no plans at all. It was a pure mistake that turned beautiful.

One foot forward... pull the other forward... How hard could that really be?

Inevitably my plans crushed my heart into fragments of what appeared to be a ruined future for myself.

September 4th, 2011:

My saliva tasted like warm milk all day but I didn't even have a drop of milk today. In fact, I've only had 568 calories today. I did 200 calories on the stairs, 105 calories on row then lifted for sixty minutes exactly. I think I'm even now. It was a good day.

October 26th, 2011:

I don't date shit real well. And this shit ain't no diary. But I date this so I'll remember the night I did something so stupid and hopefully didn't create a problem for myself or some sort of sick habit.

Tonight my feelings ran deep. I felt quiet and edgy. Mom made delicious cheeseburgers. I went barbaric and consumed a burger and some of another and then I don't know what happened. I immediately felt upset. I went upstairs and straight to my bathroom, stuck my hands down my throat and puked myself dry. The burger tasted just as good coming out as it did going in. It was that fresh. I felt fucked up. Wrong. Dumb. I knew better but I also didn't know anything at the moment. I feel weak, I can't even describe the shame I feel at this moment. Why did I? My eyes are outlined in red.

Judge me.

Sometime after this entry (not dated):

I hope to God this isn't what it seems.

I feel my life going to a dead end.

Or maybe it's a cul-de-sac.

I can't find my route out.

What the hell do I do?

Is this true?

What is this?

It tickles.

It consumes my mind with negative feelings.

Maybe.

No.

It can't be.

What do I do?

I'm scared.

November 2nd, 2011:

I'm losing my mind and I'm not quite sure that I even care to stop it.

November 4th, 2011:

Frustration is often defined in silence and today I found myself so silent it hurt. Shit just ain't always going to go the way you want. And my shit is far far away from my wants.

I want to make some good friends. I feel so left behind.

November 14th, 2011:

I ran well in my half marathon the other day but I remember binging that night on Mexican food with Cassie. When we got back to my brother's place, I tried to force myself to throw up but I couldn't do it quietly tonight so I had to sleep with my fat stomach. I hated that I couldn't fucking do my dirty sin. My routine. My purging. I needed it. I could hardly sleep with the pressure in my gut and I paid the price at mile four in the race, but somehow ran a decent time of an hour and thirty-six minutes. About half a mile away from finish line my damn sciatica nerve got pinched from one of my metal rods and I cried my eyes out all the way to completion.

November 18th, 2011:

Again.

I didn't really comprehend nor did I realize how pathetic I was until I found myself fingers crammed deep down into my throat, wiggling them in a disgusting manner, my eyes crying of shame and my stomach hurling into knots. I peed my pants due to the dramatic push to vomit. So this is what it's like. To lose control, to be weak. I couldn't get up what I just ate.. So like any bulimic expert. Wait, I'm an expert now? Fuck. But I chugged some water to liquidate my over indulgence of food. I'm sick. So sick. Mentally I was yelling profanity at myself. Stop this shit right now. This is twice today. And I'm not even fat. I am ripped and 'healthy'. I know how much nutrition I need, I know how terrible this is for me and how unsuccessful it is. I know I speak poorly of those who perform what I am doing at this very moment.

I look at my surroundings as in some kind of lame excuse. I'm puking because... And all I could come up with is... I'm puking because I am -? And that's all I got. I vow to never do this again and go back to my healthy eating habits. I can start over. I acknowledged my mistakes, I dove deep down into a vicious cycle of fear. I'm swimming my way out as a leader. I can do this. I needed to write this down, although I am painfully ashamed, I need to record this so I never have to write such dumb bullshit again. This is my one and only acceptance of faults. And never will I accept it again.

November 24th, 2011:

I took a few minutes to look for this certain pen to write with. I didn't find it so I feel almost reluctant to write, yet I have such beautiful, disturbing ideas and thoughts in my head today that I cannot resist. The pen is not an expensive, pretty one but it gets the job done, it's actually a piece with no cap. Earlier I rubbed off what I hope was coffee stains on it and despite my hesitation, this piece of shit writes smoothly, displaying just enough ink. It's almost making my handwriting come out cute and perfect like I could never cramp up with it pathetically in my hand while writing bullshit essays.

Today I realized... nothing. I coasted through classes like an air balloon soaring aimlessly. I am lost in a world that confuses me. I am my own punctuation. I can either make this end in a period or in an explanation mark. Just how exciting and cheesy do I feel?

Lately, I've devoted my mind to other things at the moment, like consuming less than 1,000 calories a day. I've come to the realization this is a mistake. I consume so little, although I know so much better. However, I like the way I've worked for this. I've neglected my temptations, my sins, my pains just like a junkie mother ignores her starving son. It tickles my mind in a sensual way almost. Like dirty foreplay that never seems to climax, cause you're constantly aching for more that you forget to just follow your heart. It becomes lust and you lose all the organically grown passion between the two of you. Your heart is then left to bubble like boiling water.

I ran the other day. Exhaling the chill of fresh air, pounding my joints into the ground. Alone. But inside... Inside of my head I replayed an imaginary fight with my best friend, whom I feel super disconnected from now. I go back and forth the arguments and I giggle to myself because it's so dramatic in my eyes.

Just how the world wants things to be makes me hate our society. It is full of self-absorbed assholes like myself. I tend to excel greatly on occasion, not cause I think I can or because I 'know' I can but because I have never once doubted myself and always pushed till I could no more. I give my all and then some. And that makes me selfish, I don't know if that's true. But that's what you called me you little bitch.

Remember, your life will excel into something outstanding if you dedicate yourself to that. To becoming better for you and those around you. But you first.

God. I really fucking wish something so violent and tragic would occur so I could get an explanation for such sad thoughts swarming my fucking head. It's fucking killing me.

I need something to record my thoughts down while I run. They are so beautiful. I want to share them but my memory gets cleaned each time I finish my stride. Why why why?

In middle school or junior high, depending on where you're from, we all call that terrible time something different. But when I was 12 years young and in sixth grade, the girls would laugh at me while I tried to play volleyball. I flew around the court like a blind zombie. So ungraceful and unattractive, falling instantly for the ball. I tried so hard but for some reason my body couldn't seem to support me. My back felt weak and paralyzed, almost as if it was stuck on some sticky tape. They laughed and called me clumsy or "O.C." for "outta control" not Orange County.

Whores. Just kidding they're okay. But really.. Whores.

It won't be until a year later I discover just why I could never hold myself up. Why my body ached so terribly and maybe, just maybe why I was so sad. I am not depressed, at least I hope so, I don't know. But I know I'm not angry. I just tend to constantly think so deeply that I get lost in the darkest cracks of my skull. Searching for new species of frog or something real exotic. Oh where might you be, you wicked creature you?

I was sad because I hurt. I was sad because every doctor told me I was fine but I just knew deep down I wasn't. It was nothing a little bit of Advil and ice could fix. I was sad because I wasn't 'pretty' or 'popular' and my back made me walk weird and cry a lot. I was sad because my Soffee Shorts didn't fit my butt like the other girls, not until my sophomore year of High School I realized that big butts were cool and a blessing. This is me bragging. My butts cool.

December 9th, 2011:

I want to be the cause of why someone got off their ass today and made something of their self.

Year 2012 was when the obsessive eating patterns really developed and I found an entire workout and food log dating every day. It details the food, calories, each exercise, and my thoughts of that day for about four months.

The average caloric intake for my days were around 950 grams with no days of rest unless I was sick.

January 20th, 2012:

Get over yourself for the damn cookies.

January 28th, 2012:

I ate a bunch of cookies, nachos, carrots. Like what the fuck. Didn't record caloric intake today. Going to bed extra early today, 7:30pm.

January 29th, 2012:

Not so great. Got ahold of some Girl Scout cookies. The end.

January 30th, 2012:

1,053 calories

143 grams protein

It's 6:35 in the morning, my eyes are burning, my saliva is absolutely disgusting, I feel disgusting inside my body. Awoke at five and haven't been able to go back to my dreams. Debated about trying to work out before physical therapy but decided it'd be too rushed. God, why am I so unworthy at this moment? Why can't I get the help to better my will and stay positive on my desired path, the one where I am successful... and alone without the demons in my head?

February 2nd, 2012:

Made poor diet choices tonight. Ate like four peanut butter and jelly sandwiches, two apples with about a jar of peanut butter too and god knows what else. My legs hurt too.

February 5th, 2012:

Superbowl Sunday... Binged on all things traditional. Sickly full tonight.

February 6th, 2012:

Not a good day on nutrition...

February 10th, 2012:

Pigged out on ice cream, protein bars. Over did it, again.

February 11th, 2012:

I ended up binging early this morning and I just couldn't stop. It controlled my entire day, even lied to my friends and said I couldn't hang out today with a lame excuse I made up. But of course I went and worked out real hard tonight. And afterwards, I stopped at a CVS and stuck my fingers down my throat and threw up everywhere in the parking lot. I started shaking and crying so hard that I fell down next to the car. Felt outrageously sick to my stomach, so wheezy and confused. The workout destroyed me too and not to mention my horrible day of food.

February 12th, 2012:

Shit just ain't so fresh. Been dumb lately. Ate freely and extremely, no workout and shamefully had a lazy day. Get your attitude back. Ate way too much and got sick last night... Tomorrow is a new day.

Committing to doing the Texas Shredder. It's all or nothing. I'm not in this to win it, I'm in it to better myself. I struggle so much with nutrition, I want to dedicate myself to curing my flaws. A sacrifice must be made for success and I need to dedicate. I need to be strong. I need to overcome my inner issues and have fun.

February 17th, 2012:

Ventured poorly :/. Same damn mistake every time.

February 19th, 2012:

Blah, blah, blah. Get yourself outta that funk and move on. Really fucking off my game.

February 26th, 2012:

Went for whack with mom's brownies.

Why do I keep making the same mistakes and feel so dumb and guilty afterwards. When shall I learn? I shall not deny my flaws, I will move on and keep my head up... Always.

You can learn great things from your mistakes... If you just learn to stop denying them and move onward.

February 28th, 2012:

Because it's all I think about. Because it's developed me into my best. Because when everyone else quits, I keep going. Because I want to help inspire others. Because I just simply, really, really want this.

March 1st, 2012:

Ate pizza. Ate zucchini bread, peanut butter, apples, apple cake, peanut butter cookies, ice cream, more pizza... Even a cup of coffee. Why.

March 2nd, 2012:

No more cheats.

No more excuses.

You obviously can't handle it...

Felt like complete shit all day. Couldn't forgive myself for eating so poorly.. Until I realized it was doing me no good to sink myself down. Got over it and every things okay now!

March 10th, 2012:

45 minute binge eat... whew :/. Very poor... very poor decisions.

March 12th, 2012:

Pretty sucky day, car insurance scene and blah upset-ness.. Went and rode for two and a half hours then messed up on meals. Just ate the world.

Really disappointing. Tomorrow is a new day. I can't believe how I acted and everything. I really did a number this time. Ultimate low.

March 22nd, 2012:

Bad Ella :(

March 21st, 2012:

After a few days of struggling, I am back on track and intend to keep it that way. :)

March 24th, 2012:

Cheat eats... Wasn't too drastic but still....

March 25th, 2012:

You know the problem. Work your hardest and to fix it.

March 27th, 2012:

Staying in control of your mind; therefore your mind cannot control your body.

Entries for that journal stop here and a new journal begins:

May 6th, 2012:

New training log. New goals. New chances and opportunities are out there. It's my moment. This is my year. I can feel it. I don't want this, I need this. It's trickling throughout my sick, dark mind. I want to better myself this year.

Status: determined to make some serious shit happen, I am committed to these words, now my actions must be disciplined and must example my attitude.

May 8th, 2012:

Just freakin' run that mountain until you puke. Weakness is a choice.

I feel disappointed in myself. I am weak. Need to get stronger. I need to stay on point; day in, day out. Make them hate.

May 9th, 2012:

What is my biggest flaw? My mind.

What is my greatest obstacle? My mind.

What is my most powerful tool? My mind.

What is my best friend? My mind.

What is my worst enemy? My mind.

What is my toughest battle? My mind.

You can choose, Ella.

May 19th, 2012:

My lack of discipline is affecting me not only physically but mentally. In my past two training logs, I have shit written down of my abusive, uncommitted habits. I really want to tweak these. I really want to become legendary. I dream of it at night. I seek it out. As if it's an injured deer, bleeding its youth out. I stalk it without blinking, licking my chops. I know how to get it, it's all about patience, it's all about belief, and hard work. I've got my dreams right in front of me. I NEED THEM. I see many quit, I see man wish. I'll do what I need to and give it my everything because it will take everything out of me to need it.

Today I ran the Spartan Sprint. A couple times I thought about quitting, each time I bent over, my back locked up, my lungs were dry and my shins were bleeding. I was poorly conditioned due to my figure show. I'm lacking endurance and stamina and I can taste it and it sure does piss me off. I got second place. I keep my head up high, as much as I thought I had this in the bag, I didn't. I don't smile for satisfaction today, I smile for the new challenge brought to my attention. I am the underdog now. I'm coming after the pain. I want to win. I will win. I am training twice as hard. I will step on toes. I am dedicated. I am sacrificing spare time with my friends. I am working after number one. Why? Cause I can and cause I have a purpose for reaching it.

June 2nd, 2012:

Sometimes it haunts me. It weighs me down, pushes me sideways, and tosses me about and not in a fun sexual way. I am practically abused by my emotions. My desire to be the very best I can be takes everything I have in me. But at the end of the day I'm often left with too many emotional mistakes, too many "what if's". No. Perfection is not my dream. My dream is to define all odds even while being lost you can still be a damn good leader. I want that. I want to be a light for others and for myself. I need it.

June 5th, 2012:

Although I am pleased with the amount of success I have worked for so far, I just wish it wasn't so lonely. I am saddened by the distance it has brought between the ones I love. The backside of them is not what I expected to see. Take me for granted and I'll be gone.

June 10th, 2012:

It is Sunday, June 10th, 2012 and my belly is tightly stuffed with trail mix and sparkling water. I feel outrageously gross, don't look at me. I don't even know who I'm talking to. Myself, myself now, myself in the future, myself in the past. Don't look at me.

Just a couple more days until I embark on my adventure to Pittsfield, Vermont for the forty-eight hour plus race that is designed to break you down mentally, physically, emotionally, and spiritually. When one asks me if I am ready, I am stuck with silence. I cannot properly define the meaning of being 'ready' for the unknown. My body aches with nerves I've never felt before and my mind has been in a constant fog, it is heavy and weary, it does not rest. However, I think I've been like this for a year now but I just can't admit it to anyone right now.

My shoulders, although now broad and thick, seem to slump down into defense with my suffering. I have been overcast with disappointment for quite some time now, I have been alone for such a good while that I now prefer my shadows. I prefer my mind even if it does suck. I acknowledge my regrets as lessons; I acknowledge my obsession as my passion. I see these things and I see others whom have given up on their dreams. I don't want to do that, I can't. I see the potential I have, it radiates. Let me grasp it, oh please let me grasp this.

I feel sick at the wastefulness the world has become adapted to, I feel somewhat ashamed of the harsh society we reside in today. I am just so tired of expectations. I don't even set that sort of limitation and stressor on myself anymore. I seek no approval, I stray from the clusters of nonsense, walk alone on my pathway to success. My pathway is so tainted it's quite amusing, how can one fall down so much, so often yet find so much success, so much growth?

I do not ask for anyone to understand me; no, no I ask only for respect. There is something beautiful about mistakes, something so beautiful about breakdowns. It hurts to mess up, to be messed up. It straight up sucks ass, so much ass and it's not good ass, you know what I mean? Nonetheless, those flaws in you slap an ego out of you, they yank you down to the ground, and yell in your face.

"HEY YOU LITTLE PIECE OF SHIT, YOU'RE A FUCKING HUMAN BEING. IT'S TIME FOR YOU TO HAVE SOMETHING TO FIGHT FOR. SHOW ME WHAT YOU'RE MADE OF AND FIGHT."

I'll cry, sure, but at the same time, I'll be starring back at that asshole's face... "Fucking give me your best, I'm not quitting." I'm in this fight for life. Sometimes I really feel like I'm fighting to live.

It's beautiful in a way that it reminds us we are alive, we are human. And in order to live a life with meaning, with passion, we must fight but fight the good fight. There is no such thing as perfection, if there was, I wouldn't want that shit. I won't even touch it with a twelve foot pole. I don't care for that amount of nothing to work for, nothing to better.

What are you if there are no flaws?

June 14th, 2012:

I have never before felt my heart's every movement so heavily. I feel weighed down, there is an atlas globe on my shoulders and I cannot balance it. My body is fatigued already, my mind still so weary, my eyes in a constant strain.

Am I prepared? Fuck, haha. I am so nervous, so anxious. I am so tired... so... so..... I am truly living. These are my emotions. I want this.

Don't think, just do.

June 15th, 2012:

When I find myself weak,

217

I will look for more.

When I find my fear's fear,

I will look at it straight into the face.

When I find myself frustrated,

I will look for wisdom in the shadows.

When I find my body failing me,

I will look for my inner strength, it's there.

When I find my mind lost,

I will look for another path onward, it's there.

June 16th, 2012:

The taste of disappointment is bitter, yet it is more appealing to me then regret. Failing is one thing, but never trying is another.

Even in the darkest of times, a light still shines. Be your own God damn beacon, Ella.

June 18th, 2012:

When the moment comes, I'll show him my scars and thank him for not making me a little bitch. And if I were to give some advice right now, it would be to find yourself a mirror and tell your reflection to suck it cause that's your only real obstacle that will make or break you. It's you.

Get over it. You've got this body, this mind.... Now get over where you're at and move onward.

I am so depressed it hurts. My leg hurts. I want to be legendary more than anything. The end. Oh, my nineteenth birthday is in three days.

June 22nd, 2012:

*Please, deliver me from my evil, however, I welcome its fearful temptations.
I smile at the challenges, don't you remember? This is my area to grow. I
feel dark and I like it... My burdens grow heavy, my shoulders grow
stronger. This is my area to grow.*

I am pleased with my success. It was all on my own. It is all me.

*There have been so many high and low points and man those low points
were extremely hard to push through. In the Death Race, I was so tired, I
could feel the stiffness in my legs cramp up as my pathetic little bloated body
stumbled that mountain all night long with that fucking tire. What am I
doing with my life? Is this the real me? I want this moment but how come I
have butchered my mind and physique leading up to this moment?*

June 24th, 2012:

*It is Monday, June 24th and I am truly disgusted with myself, my actions,
my mind lately, my situation, and majorly my physique.*

*Today marks my comeback. I sulked and allowed my emotions to take full
control of myself and I got lost. Very, very fucking lost in my doubts. It is
embarrassing and weak. It's like all that I've preached went silent in my
own head and my heart hesitated. And that's it. I've had enough. It's time.
Time to work. Time to gather the shattered pieces of my mind and get my
flow again. From here on out, no matter the temptation or how hard it gets,
I will NOT fucking fail or give in. I am much stronger than that.*

*I struggled for a couple more days but I have sat too long in my own way,
here goes nothing. Back to me. :)*

*"Without the bad days, there would be no good days. And no true
friends."*

Diary ends with this entry and I started a new one that is poorly dated. Yay
for my short attention span. I have done my best to put the dates in
properly:

August 17th, 2012:

Roads to success are twisted like candy canes.

Everyone struggles, makes mistakes, becomes negative, finds themselves lost, decides poorly, and falls down. The difference between winning and being a failure is that brief moment after you've fallen. Do you bounce back up and push through or do you lay there and sulk into the dirt? Do not be defined at how many times you have fallen or how you go down. Be defined at how you get back up and why you do so. That is, if you have the balls to. So next time you make a mistake, think negativity, find yourself lost, make a dumb choice, or fall down, remember you're a pussy if you don't get back up. Everyone who is successful once did the same thing you're doing. They pushed through to be legendary. Be the best you can be and achieve the ultimate prize of overcoming an obstacle. Get over your flaws and learn to cope from and with them. For you are human and you were designed for imperfections, you were designed to destroy something so beautiful only to recreate something more meaningful. When I reach heaven or to that magical place on the other side of life, I will thank the higher being standing before me, whether that may be God or not, I will thank him for the body of which he has given me to win.

Underdog Underbites.

They're talking negatively about you. Snickering their way with their jealous hisses, eyeing you down in a bitter envy glaze. Nodding their airless heads that are filled with their self-serving bias, explaining to themselves that they deserve this, not you.

They're speaking about your great accomplishments and tight look. Your hard work is inspiring to those around you, yet so annoying for some. Your success is spoken either way, let those who suffer in a weak cycle of jealously hate you and those who congratulate you become your motivation.

For this is your own life and you have every right to live it the way you choose. To better yourself and move on; scar tissue is tougher than regular tissue anyways.

September 1st, 2012:

Distant success within.

I am not famous nor have I done anything historically astonishing. History books will not carry my name years from now and my adventures will soon be forgotten.

I simply ask for the time being that you do not pity me or envy me. Just like every cliché story out there, just like every other individual out there I overcame an obstacle that quickly challenged me with the worst but slowly developed me into my best.

I am full of mistakes, disappointments, and sure maybe a regret here and there. But without these misfortunate routes and steps I took, I'd be gone. Somehow I've found the right way. I was never the one making newspaper headlines or setting new records. Strangers did not shout my name. I was that dim candlelight in the back of the room, while the bigger fireplace gave warmth to everybody in the room. My moment to shine will come and that with everybody else if you just learn to let go of the idea of perfection.

On occasion, we find ourselves doing unquestionable acts we normally would not participate in... Sometimes we wonder what the purpose is of our existence here on Earth. I believe we are not here for a reason or for a chance to change the world. I have a weird feeling we are all here for a lesson. We all are searching so desperately for acceptance, happiness, money, love, and the next big thing. Life is taken for granted and we need to just learn to live. Simply, live.

I stress the importance of nutrition, for it is something we all kind of struggle with. The image we'd like to have reflecting back at us is never really there. Forget those around you, that skinny bitch in the tights or the woman with the amazing quads and just focus on yourself. It is your body, it's always going to be different than those around you so stop trying to be someone or something that you're not. Focus on what it is you need to do and what you want and just go forth. Simply, live. It's a long journey so make sure you are happy with the path you have chosen.

Just ate your weight in cookies? Get over it. Tomorrow's a new day. Work harder and harder. If you're going to indulge you better put in some damn work. This will never be easy. It will be worth it. You should cry, you should question your motives but without ever doubting yourself completely. You should evolve into something much greater if you learn to just take the lesson for what it is and simply live. How successful you are depends on how dedicated you are to yourself. Life's a goal, so what're you waiting for? I didn't get here without hard work, I did not wake up successful, I did not give up on myself for nothing. No, no. I woke up by myself early in the mornings and I sprinted, I fell, I got back up, I pushed myself, alone. It was me, yelling the times in my head, telling me to pick my knees up, to go faster. I did this. You see this? I did this. And this is me. I didn't do this for you or him or them. I did it for me. I proved to myself once again that you can truly do anything if you give it your everything. With that being said, I want to be the reason someone got off their ass and made 'someday' today.

Don't just expect miracles to happen in life, make them happen. Make it legendary, make it for the history books cause just maybe, when I do die, someone will read this and actually understand me and my name will be remembered.

I don't even understand myself. I am an achy boned individual. I am lonely yet content with my boredom. I'm focused on beating second place. I'm out for my best and beyond. Every time I'm training I give it 110%, I do not have time to slack. I do not wish to be second, I wish to be the best. So I woke up one day and stopped dreaming and decided to go after it, despite its distance. I stopped my wishing and I did it.

No one wakes up and says to themselves, 'today I will fail at everything I attempt. I will quit at the first ache and that's okay.' So why are you? Why are you quitting on yourself? That ache will fade. Your pride, however, will always be altered.

My heart on occasion will ache because for the first time in my life I have felt proud of myself. I have pushed so hard and struggled through so many nights. I missed out on my childhood due to the chronic pain in my back and sometimes I just feel really high. As if this is not really me. I'm not that same girl who once carried a pillow in school. The one who was in a wheelchair and loss muscle strength at Six Flags. The one with four metal rods and six screws in her back. The girl who couldn't play sports but tried so damn hard to. The one who's spine was never connected to her sacrum since birth?

Yeah. That's me. I'm a different kind of miracle. But so is everyone else.

We are all something great, we just gotta choose to be.

Life is like an obstacle race and that's truly why I enjoy these races I do. It requires brute strength, patience, endurance, and a strong mind. All of these things I have strived for as a child and take confidence in. At times it may seem as if I am cocky, but I'd rather have me some confidence than be barring myself into a dark hole of low self-esteem. That shit's ugly.

Books are warm, like your mother's homemade pies. They're rich and hopefully unique. A bunch of words bundled into these things called 'sentences' are hard to hold my attention. Makes perfect sense as to why I enjoy writing and would like to publish a book.

My main purpose of this is to help others who are struggling in any kind of way to get back up. I don't care whether it is that you're a gay in hiding, a fallen warrior, a single mother, a wannabe athlete or a lonesome junkie, I want you to fulfill your lesson in life so that you can one day teach others in your next journey in life, wherever that may be.

My parents are your average, loving couple who give plenty for their kids. They taught me manners, responsibility, and values. Excuse my crude language, they did not teach me that, however I'm just not about to sugarcoat my expressions, I'll walk straight through that bush and grab the damn honey. I'm all about support, you see, but there are some things that need to be done alone in life. And with that being said in my opinion, finding yourself is one of them.

Let yourself get lost by yourself so that only you can find your lesson in life, your main reasoning, your purpose as to why you are being written day by day.

It's amazing how much dumb shit we remember and how many important things we forget. Although middle school isn't all that important, it was just three ugly years of my life that was ruined. Ruined by pain. Ruined by eleven year old girls. Ruined by immature relationships and school work. Ruined by surgery.

Injuries occur more often than I'd like to accept for myself. And I'll never want to admit it but it's partly my fault most times (I grit my teeth like a concerned mother would at her son's first varsity football game). I push so hard and ignore my body's jolting aches with a smirk, I just don't want to stop, I don't want to rest. But hell, I need to. Every athlete needs it. Your damages will catch up to you and you will find yourself regretting that run or that play or that lift later. Active rest is a believable tactic to use when you have a mind that is constantly pushing you forward.

I want to be an inspiration. I want to be on a poster that a young athlete mesmerizes and tells themselves "I wanna be just like her." I want all the underdogs to rise upward; I want to be the reason why so-and-so lost 200 pounds. I want to be known for my scars and for who I really am, not for my performances on the course. I want to be like my brothers and save the world. So strong and courageous. I want to be sponsored well enough that I can travel the world and share my story. To help better others and help better myself. I may be strong but we are all weak at some point. I just want that support, you see, I'm all about that.

Every day I fight. Not to just be at the top of the line, but every day I fight to be better than I was yesterday, so that tomorrow will be better, so that my future will be better, so that I will be better. Each day is a new day to get better, to set new records, to recalculate my stats, to adjust my mind, to improve in all aspects, to succeed, and to get one step closer to my goal of being the best Ella Anne Kociuba. I will be number one. Second place does not fit me, I want first. I want my best.

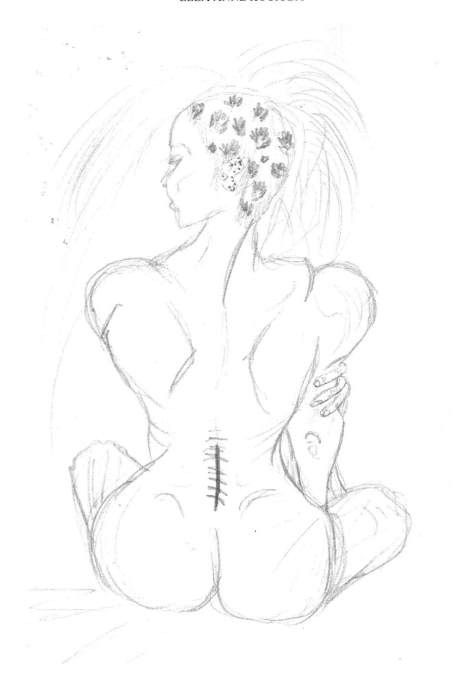

September 7th, 2012:

To be successful in my honest opinion is to stop putting so many damn expectations on yourself. Even in general, just stop expecting yourself to accomplish all these damn tasks. Instead set goals; goals of which you will eventually achieve through hard work and dedication. Start with small ones and work your way forward until you make your way to bigger things. It helps me avoid disappointment by not expecting greatness all the damn time, to not expect gold every time, and to even not expect a solid finish. I look forward in every situation because ahead of me is my goal. My goal is first place, a great finish, the best version of myself, it's everything and it's in front of me. It's in front of you. Everything I have been working so hard for is right there and we just need to keep our eyes open, let others expect things we don't know about. And let's simply live. Watch me, I'll do my thing, I'll accomplish little goal by little goal until one day, I'm someone's biggest goal.

When I finish a race, I don't end it disappointed if I miss gold, if I don't cross the line faster than everyone I wanted to, which is everyone... Haha. But I finish one step closer to my goal, you've gotta look at it this way, you've gotta find the appreciation in every situation you encounter. But shit, I better have given it my complete everything if I fail short of first.

October 13th, 2012:

The way I see it, if you're not thinking about quitting, push harder. If you are thinking about quitting, push even harder. This is what separates you from everybody else, this is your moment to reach the best version of yourself, whether that's first place or even just finishing something. It's supposed to hurt like hell, you should feel like death. That's what a barrier wants you to believe, that you're not ready for this, that you're not strong enough. This is no walk in the park, this is victory and like those before you they worked hard and long through the hard times too. You aren't different; there are plenty of others out there who are thirsty for this. Drink up.

It's not a matter of want anymore, it's a need. You need to get this. You're not going anywhere if you don't feel the exhausting desire for it. This is part of it, it's not going to be easy for you, it's going to be trying to consume your every thought from here on out, can you handle it? Can you push past the thoughts and wake up every day and perform the way you should?

Analyze what needs to be different, what you must change and what you must do. What do you need to improve on and how will you do it? Figure out whatever it is that needs to be done and just do it. This is such a long journey for you, so choose your steps wisely and make sure at the end of the day you are happy with your performances. Tie your shoes, life's a go.

October 28th, 2012:

I don't eat dough.

Many girls my age when handed money instantly think about how much booze they can get by begging their older friends to purchase it, or to go shopping for those new shoes they saw online and blow money. I, on the other hand, instantly think, okay, now I can afford that race and those new tights to compete in. My thoughts just revolve around competing; will this benefit me in the long run? Am I actually going somewhere with this?

I can't even focus in school. It's like some sort of poison for me and I'll gladly get sick off of this shit please and thank you. In my mind I am constantly analyzing each and every opportunity given to me, I view the consequences, the risks, and the work that needs to be done.

My will-power on food has grown somewhat weak and it's now a routine, I do believe, I cave in and go on terrifying binges, especially when I get below 14% body fat. My weight varies weekly but typically I have been around 127 pounds. I would like to see 120 pounds on me. I am an athlete, I am rough around the edges with a wide variety of strengths. Currently my favorite body part on myself is my arms, they are massive yet lean and hold just the right about of bulk on my lean body that I strongly hold up. My quads and shoulders are also very defined, my abdominals appear lean, yet not as shredded as I'd like at the moment. My back is very strong, for the first time in years. In general, I'd like to consider myself a brick. I do not bend, I am not easily altered and I have found my forte. It's nothing pressed onto me, I made this. I found this and I fell in love. I'm going to live in this very moment and take in everything it has to offer me.

November 10th, 2012:

I will find out that my success will cause some of my close friends to turn up their noses at me. I will be called names and get categorized as 'self-centered' and an 'adrenaline junkie'. Later, I will find out that I have a fear of eating and my appearance becomes my controlling center of attention. I will develop bad eating habits and mentally put myself down while trying to keep others up. I will find myself happy with the loneliness I embark on cause that's where I'm successful at or so it seems at the time. I will fill my downtime with writing and planning new workouts, diets, and researching my goals in a cheap notebook with my head floating. I will push through my aches until I am no longer mobile because I do not like to rest. I will feel ugly when skipping a workout due to a holiday or sickness. I will be so focused on my dreams that I will never wake up from them. I will find supplements to naturally enhance my performance and I will compare proteins with their reviews and data. I will spend money on weighted vests and workout gear. I will forget partying and go about my early bed time and morning workouts. I will come to find that this brings me happiness. I will come to find out that people close to me do not understand it and quickly judge me. I will find out that I'm good at being distant with others who damage me emotionally. I will find out that the pressure of being a role model is my biggest scare and I will crack. I will develop many injuries that will not be cured. I will become a monster in the weight room and I will force myself to puke from exhaustion. I will excel and not find satisfaction until my competitors shake my hand. I will find out that I literally will never give up on myself even if I am my own worst enemy. I will find out later that I am my own destruction. I will run away from comfort and push for more pain. I will dream of winning when I sleep and wake up and chase it. I will vision success when I am bored and even when I am busy because it is truly all I think of. I will always be planning and anticipating tomorrow's training. I will find out I am addicted and I will find out what it takes to be successful. And I will give it.

November 19th, 2012:

It always was a part of my life. It varied depending on the day's demands, but never failed to leave me suffering by the time the sun hid itself. But who am I kidding? I suffered nonstop, I ached, throbbed, and sensations that I cannot describe.

December 20th, 2012:

Dammit.

Holidays are a time for visiting family and feasting. I love being with my family, but I very much dislike the feasting.

For the longest time I was eating clean and well while keeping up with my training every day. Weak before traveling I slipped up with a bad knee injury causing me to put a sudden halt on my training. Quickly put me in a downward spiral and when offered food, I will eat it and just not stop for hours.

My healthy, lonesome routine slips away from my tight grip and my mood deepens with frustration, anger, confusion, sadness. I regret each bite and envision working out again, oh how badly I want health. I am overflowing with negativity and anticipating my well-being and the gym.

I research LCL tears and knee braces, my pain is increasing and so is my weight. I am sad but I can't let this phase me, I cannot be this weak. I am much tougher than this, I will pull through and get on the right track. My goal is too beautiful to drop on such adversity as this.

Become legendary.

Year 2013 begins, and it looks promising. But not long after its days begin it fades into the darkest times of my life.

While I did not do a very good job at dating my journals during this time, I do recall most of these terrible stories from the bruised areas in my head vividly. Here they are for you to read and also for you to learn from:

January 3rd, 2013:

I'm veering off like a drunken fool, I'm spinning out of control onto a dark path.... Again. The trees are collapsing around me. I think I get your fear now Snow White. The sudden crash in my environment is unfortunately familiar. I remember all these feelings. I remember the guilt, the painful emotions that are always played on a high note for all to hear, however, they will never actually feel it.

I'm working myself up and prepping for my downfall, don't mind me, I'm just anticipating my breakdown. I'm so nervous, I believe I jumped before the gun even went off. Disqualify me, I'm lost in the mess I've created.

February 4th, 2013:

Because a victory without struggle is no true victory at all, fight for it.

February 9th, 2013:

Still cannot get over my victory this past weekend. It was crazy beautiful. I really gave it my all. I really left it all out there. I really battled it out. I beat April by five seconds. It was so intense, I could feel the oxygen zip from my body as I sprinted towards the finish line. Screaming, my lungs tanked. It was like I always envisioned it. It was like back then, when I won my first ever race. This is it. This is my year, I'm back.

February 15th, 2013:

I'm training so hard lately, I'm killing it. I am running fast. I am so strong. So lean. I'm back. I'm so back in this. My head. My heart. I am capable of all things.

March 26th, 2013:

A couple of days ago I competed in North Carolina. I won, it was cool. Literally, super cool. About 30 something degrees and raining. All of us elites slipped off the monkey bars, the traverse walls, so many burpees, such little time. But this is beside the point; I have done something to my foot. It's not okay. I was running out at Brushy Creek when suddenly Casper, that little prick shanked the side of my foot and I collapsed down some. I limped my poor ass back the mile and half I had left. I'm worried. I race in Vegas in a couple days, and I can hardly walk.

April 10th, 2013:

I knew I shouldn't have ran on it. Got my ass kicked today. Finished like fourth or fifth or some kind of shit like that. When do I place that low? Oh, right, when I'm a dummy and run on an injury. I'm going to see the doctor soon, I cannot take the risk of this being something serious. It made me limp and bite my lip the entire eight miles this past weekend.

April 30th, 2013:

Well I'm hurt, again. Perhaps 6-8 weeks if I'm lucky. I ruptured the prevous longus and brevous tendons in my right foot. I'm still able to train legs for the most part so I will work around my injury, this will pass. But I went and got a Sonic Reese's blast to cry and eat to. I'm okay, I'll mend. This is nothing to cry about Ella Anne, you'll be back.

May 3rd, 2013:

It's always easier said than done.

May 15th, 2013:

Life is a constant battle. We are either fighting to be on top or fighting to not be on the bottom. I cannot seem to find the neutral. I don't want to prove anything. I don't need to. I just want contentment so badly.

May 25th, 2013:

I've been, for the most part, light in the head. But that beacon comes and goes, I cannot seem to keep it lit for long periods of times. It's been a couple weeks into my injury and although I stay positive, it is real annoying being here in this position.

June 13th, 2013:

My birthday is soon and I'm a fat fuck. I'm injured too. And tonight I snuck out of my window just like I used to do back in high school. I crept down the posts and carefully made my way to the pasture. The horses were sleeping peacefully in their stalls; Coca flared his nostrils as I approached him, gracefully gliding my hands across his back as I made my way past him. I see Chance out in the paddock, his eyes observing me; I come up and kiss his soft nose. I've always loved a horse's nose. It's so soft and precious, just like my heart. It's quite soft at this moment.

You know why I love horses so much? Not because of their obvious beauty and athleticism but because of the fact that they communicate through body language. They pay attention to the details, to the smallest of all things. They will respond to you and they have the strength to do great things yet they listen patiently to their owner's commands when respect is bolded.

I went down to the end of the pasture where the very few trees we have are collected. I sit down on the ground, into the fluffy dirt, it's one in the morning and there seems to be no souls awake but the creatures that roam the night. Oh how I want to be an animal sometimes. It's a bright night and I sat there in silence for a few minutes, just breathing slowly, the air feels good to my lungs. I really want to be lost. I really want to be let go of. And here comes the tears. I begin to cry and I am still so uncertain as to why I keep finding myself so sad. Is this depression? I think so. This whole eating thing is ruining my world and I feel alone in it. I'm about to be twenty and it seems like I got my shit together, sort of. But I'm just a mess and tonight I cry. Tonight I cry for all those reasons. I cry because I read online the stories from so many others saying I have inspired them but I don't even feel inspired. I feel dull. I feel lost. God damnit, I'm rambling and I still have dirt on me. I'm dirty in the truth here. And the truth is, I'm hurting and I want to be saved but don't know how to reach out.

June 20th, 2013:

Happy early birthday to me, I've eaten the whole world. And puked up my entire dignity up or so it seems...

June 29th, 2013:

I have so much to look forward to. So much that I need to be presentable for and I just can't seem to fucking grasp it. I'm fucking losing it. Let's get our shit together.

July 7th, 2013:

Today I almost killed myself. Not on purpose but by accident. My heart hurts so badly. This is getting so out of control. Perhaps I would be better off if I had just let it happen. But I couldn't let it slide down my throat any more. I couldn't let my mother find me with a fork shoved down my throat, puncturing my precious esophagus and my body lifeless. I don't want my friends to know of how sad I was when I died, I don't want my fans to see this weakness. I don't want to feel this. I don't want to be this, but why can't I shake it off? Why, oh why can't I escape you?

It was the typical binge. I splurged on everything and anything I saw, stuffed my stomach past its comfort, and then some. I got my long fork and went upstairs. As I think of this, I never really actually think too much as I walk my way to the toilet, to the place where I breakdown, to the point at which I purge until I cannot even feel my own heart. Just so numb, I go straight there, sit down in front of it casually and sit there. It always takes me a split second to prepare myself to purge.

Dangling that fork down my throat a little bit, I feel my muscles contract and resist it but I push it past the hesitation, the guard. The right thing and I go wrong. I go blind. I go dark.

I was having an abnormally odd time getting stuff to come up today. I chugged my soda to help bring up the food and still, most that came up was stomach acid and juice. In some frustration, I almost kill myself. As I put my fork back down my throat after puking up, it slides down into its place, my fingers grasping it tightly when suddenly the stomach acid on the fork causes me to loose grip of the fork. I lost it. My fingers were no longer holding the fork. The fork was sitting in my throat and about to slide down.

In my head I am freaking the fuck out but I know to stay still and calm and don't move my head one bit. I carefully but at the same time quickly put my fingers back down my throat and grasp the fork, it slides some, I'm about to lose grip, I'm about to lose my breath, I'm about to lose my life.

All I can think of is my mother, my father, my family. I don't want them to see me die like this, I don't want anyone. I don't want to die like this.

I do not know how but I managed to grasp the fork and pull it out of my throat. Immediately I cried the hardest I have ever cried before. My entire arms were shaking and my body began to sink into the floor. I curled up next to the toilet holding the fork so tightly that my fingers begin to cramp.

"I'll never do this again, I'll never do this again."

About two hours later I found myself back downstairs eating out of control and I go numb and head back up to the toilet. I sit down for my quick moment, my quick collection. And I can't seem to do it for a split second, I am sobbing so hard. I am so confused. The food comes up this time with blood, and lots of it.

I'm sure in a couple weeks, months, even years from now I will wonder to myself, what if I didn't get that fork, if I didn't get a grasp of it, if I died right then and there from getting that fork lodged into my throat...

What if?

The day Brownie died, and the days after it, I tried to journal about my feelings and thoughts but decided to suppress them and move away from that memory. Therefore, I have no journal entries about the death of my dog. I wanted to pretend it never happened.

July 12th, 2013:

When I look in the mirror I don't even know who I see anymore. I've been waking up every day and all I do is eat, eat a fuck ton. I just fucking eat and can't stop. I go puke it up then go back downstairs and eat again. That sounds a little funny, 'I can't stop eating' but I'm serious. I'm so fucking serious. It's controlling me. I'm trapping myself into my house and it's terrifying. I fear the gym for I look nothing like I usually do. I am heavy. I am not confident. I am so sick and tired of this.

July 14th, 2013:

What a good trend going on here, all I have to say about myself is 'I'm fat' 'I can't stop eating' 'I feel sad' 'I'm so confused'... Even if I don't understand, I just want someone to understand me. I just really want to be held. I miss being loved. I miss true affection; I want to give my heart to someone. I want to be the reason they go to sleep and wake up happy... And I want that. I want to feel happiness. It's hard to force it onto myself while inside I hurt so much. Someone come find me.

Ahhh-haha. I'm not desperate, I swear. Or am I?

July 18th, 2013:

Been 'clean' for four days so far, my mind feels good! Meals are good, training is what I can do, still a bit injured.

July 21st, 2013:

So I took some steps forward and then I fell backwards like a huge fucking hippo that I am. Really dug myself into some deep calories today. I fucking hate myself. But I can do this.

July 23rd, 2013:

I'M JUST SO FUCKING FAT. I CANNOT STAND HOW I FEEL, HOW I LOOK, AND HOW MY LIFE IS CURRENTLY.

And only I hold the power to change it all. It is I who must make sacrifices, put the hard work in, and push out the negativity. I know how to do it and how to get there. It's time to go back. Back to my happiness, back to me, back to lean, back to life as it should be.

GET YOUR SHIT TOGETHER. REMEMBER HOW DISGUSTING YOU FEEL AND LOOK RIGHT NOW AND LET'S FUCKING CHANGE IT FOR THE BETTER.

July 27th, 2013:

New project: make some workout books. This should inspire me to get back to my old roots but in a smarter way.

July 28th, 2013:

In a few days I go on tour. I'm not by any means the Ella I should be, the Ella that I am, I am far from it. I am soft. I am heavy. I am sad. I am quiet. I am confused. I am awkward. I am uncomfortable. I am all these foreign things to myself that I am so scared and nervous to go on tour. But fuck, I can't do much about it now.

From August 1st to August 4th, I was on tour with my first sponsors on the East Coast. When I returned to my home in Texas, my sadness deepened and settled itself further into my chest.

Although I did not journal during the time I was on tour, I can recall just how quiet and how sad I felt during the experience. I was terribly embarrassed of my body but I tried my hardest to act as if everything was okay, as if I was okay. But really, I wanted help so bad… So fucking bad.

August 19th, 2013:

College makes me sad and I'm not even at a real university. I am at a community college, let's add that to my no real friends, food controlling, body swelling, training around the clock, injured as hell life that I got going on.

Wow, that was dramatic. My life isn't that bad, I can turn this around. I'll smile. I can do this.

My most recent diary and up to date until publication of this book:

January 2nd, 2014:

When's your first race back?

When will you compete again?

Are you ever going to compete again?

How do you keep going?

SHUT UP, fuck.

I've got so many goals; trust me. It blows my mind and I will be achieving them.

Emotions are silly. Do not think, just do. This is your chance, your time. Throw it away or own it Ella, but whatever you do, just do it already.

Feed me doubt.

January 4th, 2014:

The other day I saw someone with a shirt on that said 'fear failure', and I couldn't help but think to myself how stupid that is. Failure isn't as negative as we make it out to be. It's an opportunity. Just like defeat is, it's fucking magical shit, okay. And if you can't see that, then I'm sorry.

No I'm not, I'm not sorry you don't have the courage to suffer and suffer quietly. Be better than shit.

Bite your lip; swallow.

I encourage you, fear, I encourage you, doubt. Come to me, try to beat me down, you may never break me. You will put me in my place from time to time, but I will always get back cause deep down inside me I have the courage to do so.

We need to stop fearing 'fear', we need to stop running away from 'doubt', we need to go after these challenges and learn something about ourselves. My body may be able to embrace the pain, but can my mind? YES. Work on it, always.

My enemy.

My best friend.

Break me.

Mold me.

Challenge me.

Fear is nothing to be afraid of, I want that cold shake, that hesitation, I want to conquer it and overcome. Fear is nothing but an emotion but without fear there would be nothing.

EMBRACE THAT SHIT.

Fear me.

Fear my mind.

I will conquer it all.

I cannot wait to compete again.

There always comes a time when words don't mean shit anymore, it will be too late to talk. Your actions will define you loud and clear. Clear your throat because I'll make you swallow your words.

January 5th, 2014:

This man at Whole Foods today talked to me while my face was naked and pale, my eyes dull, hair wet, clothes baggy. He talked to me as if I was a unicorn or an angel. His eyes glistened. I feel like I could see my reflection with his admiration for my statue. It was magically flattering and I was satisfied that even with my rough demeanor I can still attract inspiration.

I have cobwebs in my head though, I don't think he saw that.

January 7th, 2014:

"It's not your time at the top that people love about you, it's your rise up."

I was talking with Dennis the other day about my first race back. Makes me feel sick and so nervous. The expectations. Eyes. Pressure. Aches. Speed. The worries are heavy and I don't know why I'm so paranoid. February 15th is my expected return and that's about four weeks from now...

Just kidding, just decided to do Extreme Nation on February 8th with three solid athletes and friends. It's crunch time now. No fucking around.

Cannot wait to grind my teeth at the start line and do some work. I must remind myself what I once did many, many years ago.

"And then one day... I was so tired of dreaming about it, so I went after it, despite its distance." There's always going to be a first. Don't think, just

do it.

One of the hardest things to do once you return back to training after an injury is to forget about old stats and make new, better ones.

Go away ego.

Go away ego.

I can recall how fast I was.

I can recall how strong I was.

I can recall all the races I have won.

BUT I'M GOING TO MAKE THIS EVEN BETTER.

January 10th, 2014:

FRESH IN THE MIND. FRESH IN THE ACHES.

To start things off, I misjudged my traveling time to arrive at Zilker Park at 9pm this past Friday. I forgot my gloves, had to park far away, I mean like all the way down at the bridge. So I was immediately overwhelmed with stress and frustration, I just chugged a coffee and an entire liter of pineapple pedialyte (solid flavor by the way). I had to pee so bad so I just squatted like a dog right there on the pavement, splash effect to the max. It's the devil's sprinkler.

My ruck was already slamming my back into all the wrong places as I tried to run as fast as I could to the start of the park where checkpoint was. When I got there I saw that there was no one there but some emo couple making out, I yelled at them breathlessly "you see some people with backpacks on?" They just stare at me, "DID YOU SEE A GROUP OF PEOPLE?!", finally they respond and tell me no. I start to freak out.

I yell out "GORUCK! CADRE, SHIT BALLS I'M HERE!"

Damnit, damnit, damnit.

I run around all mad-like, I'm aimlessly trotting around the field in the dark, yelling out cuss words and screaming for the cadre. When finally I hear a response, they're over by the rocks, I smiled like a fool as I run over to them in a giggle.

Cadre yells my name and tells me to drop my shit. I do so.

Shut up.

Army crawl to me.

I crawl over to him.

Now crawl backwards.

I crawl backwards.

Get up, Kociuba.

The cadre is Big Daddy, this outta be good.

I nod to myself, I am here for my breakdown, so happy, for I can become quiet tonight and so the night begins as we head over to Barton Springs. We are told to enter the cold water where it rises to mid-calf.

Bring on the shakes.

We get hazed for about an hour or more.

I tried so hard to focus and count the sets and reps of our torture but the water was splitting my ribcage open.

"Do you fear water?"

What is fear? I tried to reason with my emotions, as if they were a con-artist, I know your tricks, I know your games. I do not fear you.

This is as accurate as my mind tells me it went:

On dry land:

- *30 pushups*
- *30 squats*
- *30 crunches*
- *30 pushups*
- *10 burpees*

About four cycles of this.

Cadre looks over at us, "you're comfortable. Ella, lead them to the water."

I steadily go in as the group follows me one by one, we get into a 360 fashion and stand in attention.

Lay on your bellies.

Gasp.

Pen needles.

Abdominals draw in.

Hair spikes up.

Goosebumps rise to the surface.

The cold is here.

You are here.

Did I mention it's thirty something outside? Or maybe it's in the forties, regardless the water is cold as hell.

In the water:

- *30 pushups*

- *30 squats*

- *10 burpees*

- *10 flutter kicks*

We do this about ten times.

We are then introduced to 'bottom samples'.

One Mississippi... Two Mississippi... All the way to ten with your entire head submerged into the water. Breathe in the light you big pussy.

Your lungs are already exhausted from the PT by now so at first I feel myself struggle. I cannot seem to bare the cold water and lack of oxygen. It's loud here.

Oh, but there is so much air in there it's not even funny, stop your gasping.

We do more pushups, I cannot forget to mention that every time you went down from the pushup you had to submerge your entire body into the water.

Pay attention to detail.

I have begun to shake uncontrollably, the current is also so strong that it pushes my frame like it's a piece of trash. I have dirt and sand somehow still stuck on my back that's being chiseled into my flesh from my ruck. Which is about forty pounds; I always use the big bricks for more weight. Yeah, that challenge.

So here we are, doing bottom samples in the water, Cadre splashing water in our faces, BREATHE IN THE LIGHTNESS, OUT THE DARKNESS.

I get up from doing a bottom sample and hear just want I love to hear.

"Don't you go to your happy place, you be here, right now, embrace this moment for what it is... Suck ass."

DO YOU FEAR WATER?

Back into the water with my face, calmer than ever, I have no happy place.

My life?

Going from burpees to crab walks to rolling around and then to more crawling.

I pee in the water, ah that's warm but not for long.

Stand up.

Get back on your stomachs.

Stand up.

Get on your bellies.

Stand up.

DO YOU FEAR WATER?

Since Cadre knew me, I got special treatment, not necessarily meaning something nice or easy. No, never, I was a target and to be honest, I sort of like it. Give me more to ache about.

We get blasted on the dry land, doing two minute max testing on pushups and sit-ups.

My body is taxed now.

My chest isn't talking to my brain.

The muscles are too busy quivering.

I need warmth.

The wind is blowing in my face, I'm soaked as I look into my bag to get my dry baggie out. Shit, it broke. All my warm gear is wet, I have nothing to warm myself with.

Way to go Ella.

"Drop your food. Give it to me. You get to eat when I say so."

We dump all our protein bars, peanut butter packets, gels.

Bye bye calories.

We go about marching, it's getting harder for me now, how could I have not rolled my dry baggie good enough? Embrace it.

But my body temperature cannot seem to keep up.

We get to a point in the trail where Cadre finds two big logs, we all come together and struggle as we carry it upon our shoulders. We must keep a one arm distance or we get a casualty, man I hate having to carry people. I've done it so many times before, it's always such an awkward effort when they're bigger than you.

Moaning, we go forth in the cold night.

I am the only female and the youngest by at least seven years are so.

Marching, we lose our right shoes.

Buddy carries bring me giggles, I coast, it is enjoyable, the sun starts to come up finally. But our smiles all turn into sick chuckles and frowns as we walk up next to a Wendy's. Cadre sees a guy hosing off the road, he asks, may I?

Line up.

Hosed in the face.

I am back to fighting my body temperature.

Shake, shake, shake.

Bite my lip, swallow, let me appreciate the good.

We go another ten or so blocks, we get hazed periodically with more bear crawls and flutter kicks.

We get underneath the bridge, get into the water.

It's gotta be 8am now.

The water bites your skin, we submerge ourselves and go about our bottom samples, flutter kicks, pushups, roll to the right, roll to the left.

Rucks above your head.

Flutter kicks.

It's real cold man.

Big daddy begins to explain to us, "I cannot make you feel sad, cold, weak. That is all you. You control this."

I earned my patch after 17.4 miles and 13 hours.

New brothers, new boundaries.

January 15th, 2014:

I had the shits while training today, I just couldn't get into it. I had to keep running to the restroom, sick as dog, hot sweats, volcanos going off inside me and you know why? Because I drank a dieter's tea this morning because I ate a big meal last night and felt guilty. I really need to stop doing that, feeling so guilty for just eating.

January 20th, 2014:

Winning is nice, sure but the simple knowledge of knowing what you had to do to get to a certain level is unbeatable.

Only you know the time you put in, the sacrifices you had to make, going to bed early, waking up early, eating right… Struggling, overcoming. It's burned into your memory now, whether you take home that first place medal or not, you are a champion in your own right.

Always work for you not just for some hardware.

February 6th, 2014:

Will I be happy if I die today?

Will I be okay if I die today?

Well, will I?

You've got to eventually ask yourself these type of questions, are you doing what you truly want, are you truly happy with yourself and the life you lead? You've got to give your life some meaning and there's nothing like knowing there's an ending near to push you into developing a new beginning.

I used to fear death.

Death used to be fearful.

But at the same time attractive.

Now, well now it is annoying.

It's overrated, you know why?

We all die. We all go into nothing one day.

So let's stop fearing the inevitable and let's just be.

Let's embrace.

Let's live.

I don't think you fully understand nor do you realize the story that's being written here. It's not about the medals, the titles, achieving a fit body, gaining a following. None of that, no. It's about failing and struggling. It's about fighting for more, it's about having the courage to stand out, to reach out, to be open, to be you. It's wanting more and going out and getting it, it's about losing fear of failure or having an obstacle get in your way. It's welcoming adversity because you can overcome it, it's the imperfections that have that make you attractive, it's enduring the uncomfortable only to recreate a new comfort. You achieve peace, sanity because you have once hit rock bottom, you have fully lived, you fell on your face time after time but you did not once quit. You got back up, you didn't chase a medal, you didn't praise the glam, you simply worked until you became you're very own hero. It's making your dreams happen even through the quiet, dark times that nobody likes to admit to but you do. You are different, you accept that and you make it happen.

It's not for popularity, it's not for that thing people call 'perfection', I do not ache for any of these things, I care for much more than what's surrounding my interior. I want to go deeper than that because I ache for a meaning. I ache to be away, to be me with no shame, so watch me rise or ignore me, whichever way you choose, I will continue to do me. I will fall down repeatedly, breakdown, and even doubt myself because I am not afraid to be human. I am not afraid to have flaws that can always use some work, I am imperfect.

Doubt, it's all around us.

Potential, it's all around us.

February 9th, 2014:

I'm on the plane. Middle seat. A slave between strangers, I'm also a burden, a barrier between personal spaces already invaded. I am a bitch.

Beast A La Mode, my team: Rachel Phuckoff, Karlee Whipple, and Cassidy Watton.

We won first place, $8,000, cool shit.

It was about 1.6 miles with twenty obstacles all clustered together just about all in front of the small crowd to witness. I overrate the two days before this, just binging on everything. I was bloated, sluggish and quite frankly, I'm still out of shape.

Although as a team we won, I am not pleased with my performance whatsoever, my God was that embarrassing, it was like I was an old, rustic piece of furniture displayed in a modern home.

Dust me off.

Oil my joints.

Touch up my paint.

I need a reminder.

On a brighter note, it was slightly overwhelming the amount of love, support, encouragement, and good vibes from everyone. So many people wished me well.

I wish I could give back more than I have, I want to cry sometimes, my fans have helped me get here, I was in such a dark place not too long ago, it was hard to change my mind but knowing I had so many people love me, helped transition that.

I'm still binging.

February 11th, 2014:

I cried so hard today. So hard that for a brief moment I grew a slight smile in disbelieve. It felt so weird to be in so much self-induced pain. Surely this is fake? Pitiful, if you may. Sobbing there in my Mother's car with my loud and out of control sobs. My eyes deep into the palms of my hands as snot and tears streamed down my face, the pressure in my gut making me feel sicker and disgusting in my own beloved body. Pitiful, if you may.

I hate the fact that I'm here again in this emotional moment. I've been here many times in the past and I hated those times too. I thought I learned, I know better and this little fact makes me feel sicker.

How was this possible? Why am I here? AGAIN. Pitiful, if you may.

I have things to be joyous about. This makes me sick. I have no reason, no excuses. I just simply lost control and didn't put all my effort to get back control to stop it. Numb to the sickness in my gut until suddenly I'm sick. So sick. I can't take this anymore.

February 14th, 2014:

To the world I am nothing but a grain of sand in your shoe, that annoying little specimen that you can't seem to find, no matter how hard you look but still you know something unique is in there, somewhere. That's me. I'm there, I'm somewhere in this world trying to get you to look around at what's to become of you.

February 22nd, 2014:

I'm just over it. Over trying to impress people and get a pat on my back only to see other's backs. I'm just so over these egos, the medals, the drama. Impressed by me or not, I'm just going to do what makes me tick. Tick tock, I don't even care to impress my own self at times.

Bite me.

March 4th, 2014:

At the time sticking that fork down my throat to rid of my sorrows felt normal, it felt routine. All of it, the intense pressure of the fork scraping against the back of my throat, the pulsing aches of guilt spilling from my eyes, and my gut pushing against my skin. And at the time, I didn't know what exactly the saddest part of my situation was. The fact that I knew better, that I was here, right now doing this to myself or the fact that I live in a society where the pressure to be perfect can crack some of the most courageously gifted souls. That the way to be successful is always hard and painful, that we should fear easiness and failure. But that's not it. We shouldn't suffer so much internally only to achieve some superficial appearance. There's a better way to live a happier and more importantly a healthier life. I want to see the change I've needed for so long, the change in acceptance of who we are for who we are, the beauty in our flaws, the lessening of pressure to find perfection and become it, the courage to be completely yourself, and the desire to grow as not only a product of this world but a product of your own beautiful ideas.... And at this time, I remembered thinking to myself, I'm already worth it. I set the fork down next to the toilet and went and trained. In a chemical way I destroyed the bad toxins in my head, while I know they will return, today I have found the strength. So many others need this reminder, because I sure as hell need it.

May 1st, 2014:

This pencil is so metal, writes so smooth, I like you.

I am a bitch again, I am a grain of sand lost in your shoes, I am that small hole in your favorite pair of socks, that dried booger that you cannot pick because you are in public.

I am middle seat on this flight again, headed to San Fran but my final destination is Burbank, California.

What for?

A 30 HOUR RACE.

But as time drags on or is it flying by- ah haaaa, I've come to a....... Fuck you eraser, sucks. I've come to a realization that I do these things not just because I love to compete but also because I want to grow as a person. I want personal growth, that's what I really ache for.

Not for glorification in my performance.

Not for a fancy medal or big fake check.

No, for me.

I do it for me, this is my personal investment. This is me being a student, although, I never really cared for academics, but boy do I care for learning about being a better person and bettering others while doing so.

Live a better life.

There is something so beautiful about a breakdown, I'm so attracted to it. It's not that I enjoy seeing others in pain or pain itself, well, perhaps I do, but regardless of that, a breakdown is beautiful because to me it is in those moments of pure agony where you truly discover yourself.

Where you can grow.

Where you can learn.

Where you can break.

Where you can just be.

You learn to appreciate the little things.

Look at the sky, there shines the sun, there hangs the clouds, feel the warmth of the rays, the cool of the shadows.

Feel your heart beat, thank you for this life, thank you for my challenges, thank you for letting me be present, I am ready, I am always worthy.

Building a better mind, one ache at a time (I need to trademark that quote, it's so fantastic, it's so me).

I want to be broken down sometimes.

I don't want to miss out on any emotion, I want to be fully present and I don't want to coast through life, I want to feel regret knotting up my guts when I screw up, I want to hear my lungs deplete of oxygen when I am exhausted, I want to feel my heart crack when someone breaks it, I want to feel strength surge through my muscle fibers as I grow, I want to feel my nerve impulses radiate when I am excited, anxious, happy, angry, nervous, or sad, I want to feel love curl my toes up, I just want to live a life so full of life it hurts, I want to stop becoming so numb.

I hope that minds start to engage in the darkness more, that within our own personal struggles, we see that the brightest moments of our lives can be found in the darkest room, just look with your heart and in those moments, you forget your hormones, your emotions, they're swaying, you're about to discover your true self. Not the bullshit you tell your friends, your families, strangers, or even yourself, you're going past the cyton in your neuron transmitters cause no hormones are going to sway you now, are you embracing this yet? This is your chance, to strip away all the fascia, all the superficial stuff, and look at your muscles in the dark.

Is this how strong I really am? Can I fight after being so exposed?

Talo: the final ending.

I hope my arteries are ready for this, I hope my heart is worthy of the poison my veins are feeding it. This poison? I'm not too sure what it is, but it pumps plasma so violently that I cannot seem to stand it, my own fingers anticipate to grip even when there is nothing there.

I'm crazy, sure, majority of the shit I do or even think, others do not dare, but I like it this way. This way of no path but this path is filled with love and good intentions; I am not evil even when there is evil within me.

All of my horses are short and I like it that way, my victories are not flashy, they are done in the quiet, when my tears fill my eyes, when my back screams at me, my legs tire, when I cannot go on but do. I am invincible in my most vulnerable state, I am comfortable in the uncomfortable because I choose to be. Tell yourself these things, tell yourself you are alright, you don't have it that bad, work hard, love yourself and you will grow into what it is that you desire.

Oh baby, the bad times are my good times too.

June 6th, 2014:

Let me get lost right now, I am headed to New York for Tri-State Spartan Race and I'm not even 'oorah-ish' about this lame shit… Okay it's not that lame, I just am so off right now. Finding myself struggling quite a bit yet again and I absolutely hate it, so much. It aches so badly, everywhere within me, I want so desperately to be free of it.

At least on this flight, I'm no middle seat asshole, I'm caved next to a window, right behind first class so I have extra leg room (score) but it's not like that really matters, I'm a short stack.

So I lost control for two days and the week before that was three days, plus some sort of virus with allergies had me down, just off.

I have slept on this flight for only 55 minutes, how disappointing, I am exhausted and this two hour and forty minute flight is dragging.

I just need some closure.

July 13th, 2014:

I really want to control this, this pain, this confusion, it's all wrapped up in thorns, piercing everything it touches. My heart, my soul, my head, I can't stand this.

Why does my head go there?

Why does my heart hide?

July 15th, 2014:

I think I'm sick in the head.

It's an illness I want to deny.

It's quite controlling.

I think it makes me beautiful at the same time though.

August 3rd, 2014:

Sometimes, I really wish my head didn't talk so loudly, I wish my head wasn't so loud with the bad. I fight it so much but I don't always win. I want to know why, why this is here.

August 4th, 2014:

Be grateful for what you have, it's someone else's dream.

Believe it or not, you got something others want.

August 17th, 2014:

Acknowledge the risk but take it anyways, understand it for its uncertainty and its consequences, but be brave.

September 16th, 2014:

En route to Team Death Race held at, of course, Pittsfield, Vermont.

TEAM EVER:

- *Luke Gregory.*

- *Brandon Welling.*

- *Patrick Mies.*

- *Ella Kociuba.*

My mind has been weary for quite some time, relapsing since Summer Death Race (June 28th). Lost myself. Lost my battle on pre-race, I will not lose this battle and I will fight so fucking hard after this race, this race...

Please release me from my darkest of dark demons. Fuck I am so ready. Break me down.

October 4th, 2014:

Be grateful for your shoes.

Make your Goddamn bed.

I wouldn't mind a beautiful tragedy.

October 23rd, 2014:

I'm a monster and it's pretty entertaining to see just how many people I've fooled by getting them to believe I was so sane, that I was in fact this thing they called 'healthy'.

Ah-haha, I'm fucking crazy.

Evil brain, angel heart.

November 2nd, 2014:

I've been real shitty with many and almost all aspects of my life.

- *Friends*

- *Training*

- *Myself*

- *Diet*

- *My room*

- *Journaling*

- *Finances*

Been eating like my bulimic self again, I'll always be bulimic. I will ditch these behaviors and let go of my pain, one day.

Today I want to reflect.

I'm really annoyed with that pen and feel very forceful with my all caps writing...

So, hello pencil.

Hello chance to erase my mistakes.

Hello to my opportunity to be fake.

And really fuckin' raw.

My problems are real,

My eating disorder(s) are very real.

My health issues are so real,

My life is in real danger.

I'm dangerous.

This relapse is a real mind fuck. It's so disturbing that I could get this lost and sad, time after time. WEAK WEAK WEAK. Ella.

My therapist, fuckin' a, I'm 21 and I have a shrink.

She says I need to stop being so hard on myself. I agree, but these habits have no thought process to them, I'm sort of a machine in many ways. It's as if bulimia is a muscle, I trained it for three years now, daily I trained the hell out of it. It wants to perform, it's strong, I don't even have to think about it, I just have to let go and letting go is real fuckin' easy. Well, sometimes, depending on the situation.

Can I let go?

Driving myself crazy.

Forever tainted, not haunted.

Drink the water.

Expression.

I am my biggest burden,

Look at these walls I climb.

See me veer away.

These dreams are kind of dying.

For my aches,

I sit in sorrow....

I want to be weightless.

I know what I need to do.

FORGET THIS WHOLE BLACK AND WHITE, ALL OR NOTHING MENTALITY.

If I eat some extra peanut butter or salmon, don't know the exact macros of a meal, it's okay, shit's not ruined.

HEAD LIGHT.

20% of eating disorder patients die.

HEART FAILURE

ORGAN FAILURE

MALNUTRITION

SUICIDE

Eating disorders are the leader in mental disorder morality rates... Way to be a leader!

Shit.

I noticed that I have begun to narrate my life in my head more. Even writing that I was all like:

"Inside your own fucked up head you bluntly speak of simple shit you do..."

What's sad here?

Me.

I have developed intimacy issues due to the harsh fact that I don't even love myself. I'm trying to let that ugly thought go. But it's just so scary how easy it is for me to block out pain, shut off others, move on, emotionally detach myself. I'm twisted.

Let's love each hour.

Let's love each curve.

I'M TRYING TO GET BACK TO JOURNALING.

I used to be so silly good at recording my daily thoughts, let's get my head straight.

I've been slippin' bad lately, binging on nonsense and while doing so I'm recalling my tactics and damnit this pen just shit the bed for a moment's notice, okay it works now, but anyways, I've been ignoring my shrink's advice, her words, my own heart and just returning to my numb old ways.

I've cried many times saying, 'I'm tired of this' and I truly am but it is so hard to go to health, to be something better than sick. That's even sick to admit. I'm so unaware of what that's like, how pathetic is that? Meh, stop beating yourself up, you're beautiful. Sure, right now you don't find your appearance to be pleasing but you're still Ella, don't lose yourself.

Be nice to yourself, don't expect to get over this or change these behaviors in one day, one week, it will take time and a lot out of you. Just like you wanted to lose weight overnight, you can't fix your mind in one night. I believe in you, I believe in myself.

November 3rd, 2014:

Woke up, ate some protein and fat, I had the urge to eat more but I resisted. So I went and did stairs for thirty minutes, sweat, sweat, sweat.

Start to this change: SO FAR FREAKIN' AWESOME!

Really want to get to the Ella I love so much and I will, I do love me now, this is all a process, EMBRACE IT.

I am as wise as the decaying bones and as free as the mangled flesh dangling off the dead.

November 4th, 2014:

Yesterday was so good, I won my battles, trained real hard, I'm happy.

Just finished running some hill sprints, felt pretty good doing so but I actually really wanted to skip my morning training.

Bitter.

But pushed it aside and killed it.

November 10th, 2014:

I think my boobs are growing, I was a jigglin' them in the shower, grabbing them, they're so sensitive and full, told myself, love yourself, Ella. Love what you have while you work on yourself.

But why is that so challenging for me?

This is the last of my journaling for 2014.

I began to sporadically write this book in 2010 but didn't get serious about actually getting it published until 2014 when I finally decided to dedicate hours a day to it finish it. From August 2014 to the day I finally finished it, I would fall asleep just about every night in my bed with my laptop on my stomach. I wrote until I fell asleep. I was determined to publish this. Even when I was in middle school I told my teachers and family that I would one day write a book, well look at me now, I did it even though my story isn't all that light.

For the most part, throughout my life so far, I have kept good accounts of my daily thoughts when they came to me in notebooks and have continued to do so but I end this section with the last of my writings in 2014.

Now it's fair to say that all I have ever truly ached for so far in life is to be delivered from my pain, to be released from the chains which restrained me from my very own potential, and simply to be something great. Within the first twenty-one years of my life I have withstood some strong currents, explored deep into the ocean's abyss, and discovered new shores to explore and man I cannot wait for more.

CHAPTER 6
BREATHE

My final words.

Deliverance (noun):

The action of being rescued or set free: "prayers for deliverance".

- Oxford American Writer's Dictionary

Mentally strung.

Physically done.

What have I become?

My recap of my life so far.

Life is different now, I am no longer completely absorbed by my darkness but I am not completely away from it, nor do I ever expect to be. Some days are harder than others and some days are easier than others, it is something that I can never forget.

I am as dark of a creature as I am light and it is the darkness that gives me my light. Yeah, I'm grateful for my hardships. As much pain as it has brought me, I do not regret my decisions in life because it is they that have essentially made me who I am, even though they caused such self-doubt and harm. They also gave me wisdom beyond my years, the courage to be my true self, the strength to never back out of my battles, a mind so open to challenges that it often aches for them.

Without these lessons I would not be Ella. Now if I look at them in a dim light, the damage shows clearly just how negative my life can be. Due to my actions my health has taken a huge toll, my mind is hindered in so many ways that sometimes I cannot seem to grasp it. I struggle with depression, bulimia, chronic back pain, hormonal imbalances, and with all these little lagging injuries that just don't seem to go away but that is life, it is hard, unfair, and we often learn the hard way but regardless of how you do it, you'll find out what you're truly made of through tough times.

My past still says hello to me from time to time, and to this day I cannot use our long smooth forks to eat because they remind me too much of my dirty habits. So instead I use the smaller forks in the drawer. It's odd how the past can shape your future and at first I didn't register that change until I noticed the weight of the long smooth forks in my hands troubling me. Although it taunts me, I've slowly learned to not be so ashamed of myself and move on with a smile.

I keep putting on a good jacket; I'm doing what I need to and then some.

As I grow more and more every day into the creature that I ached so badly to be, I've come to terms of what it is that I'm truly grateful for. Believe it or not it is the shitty times that I find myself thanking life for. I blame them for my success, they certainly take credit for being the reason why I am the way I am, and they definitely made me unstoppable inside my mind, even at times of pure hurt.

Now I ask you, do you feel it?

More importantly, do you see it?

Success can made from failures.

Negatives can be positives.

It's a matter of perception.

It's a matter of actions.

Do I have your attention yet?

Do you think I'm crazy yet?

Well to be honest, you've got to be a little crazy to want to do crazy things and I don't seem to mind that I lost my mind long ago in the midst of my own misery. However, it's actually quite beautiful to have had the opportunity to experience such grit building, soul discovering challenges, but, my heart goes out to anyone who feels or has felt the way that I once did.

I wrote this for you, I wrote this for me, let's be a beacon for ourselves.

Someone great once told me that some of the most incredible people you will meet in your life are also some of the most fucked up people, I want to say that I am living proof of this statement and I'm not even ashamed to say I've got a few screws loose, who doesn't?

We live in a society that preaches 'no pain, no gain'. We live where beauty is often defined by having no wrinkles and long eye lashes, where a tanned, skinny body is admirable. It seems that our world praises the abuse of power, money, and love. Our vision becomes superficial and before we know it we are drowning in our sorrowful moods about life itself. We often forget that somebody out there has it worse and that we should be grateful for what we have… Like the shoes on our feet.

Yeah sure, walk a mile in someone else's shoes, but sometimes they don't own shoes.

Quite frequently I remember the soft tennis balls on my walker back in the hospital when I was thirteen years old. That memory reminds me that sometimes our lives can be stripped away from us in a blink of an eye, and all the simple things that we take for granted can become severally complicated… Like forks.

So don't you dare forget to love your life even if all you have is a jacket upon your shoulders. Go ahead and look down into your hands, force good change upon yourself. You're going to be okay, somebody's got it worse than you.

Bite your lip; swallow.

This is the first of many books to come. As I wrote this, I found it to be incredibly therapeutic to my body, yet extremely traumatizing to my mind and heart due to suppressing the majority of these memories inside the smallest, darkest parts of my little head. Digging them out was a painful process filled with a mixture of 'this is going to be great, this is going to change the world' or 'I don't want the world to see this, my mother doesn't even know this shit' and while at times I wanted to give up on it, I didn't.

I can remember vividly crying and screaming for a breakdown all the time, for something to fall apart on me, for a definite reason as to why I was in so much pain. While I scrambled through the emotions, I found myself absorbed by them all. Oh they were so heavy, I could feel the insertions of them but not their origins

Where was the pain and this sadness coming from?

And then I remembered… I remembered falling off of Socks that evening and the darkness I saw that night was just the beginning of my downward fall. It is also in that moment where it became my vision and it instilled itself as the origin of my entire life.

Back then I accepted life as pain and pain was my life. However, even though I agreed to that outlook and truly believed it, I was dramatically incorrect. Just because my life was a challenge didn't mean I had to allow it to be.

Change is the one thing that is always present in our lives and in this situation; it is in my favor to force it upon myself.

With any type of difficulty you face in life, you first must find out where it comes from in order to ease it. Notice, I don't say 'fix it', because sometimes not everything can be fixed, but they can be controlled, managed, and even altered to an extent.

Once you find the direction it's all up to you to go forth and make peace with it. Now, while on your journey I can guarantee that you will get lost countless of times, you will trip over yourself or others like a drunken fool and fall onto your face. You will even feel like it's not worth it and want to quit, you will also fear comfort itself even though you scream for it when you're alone. You're going to go through this phase many, many times and sometimes you will get to the origin, put it on pause but then find it blaring back in your head, oh would you look at that, it's time to go on another trek.

It's an addiction that has created you, it's a drug that you so pathetically consume, it's you and you can't let it go without a fight even if it's killing you. This pain you feel is all a part of a withdrawal to something so powerful that we cannot afford to bottle it up nor can we even begin to understand it but you must put change upon yourself, especially if your life and sanity are threatened.

Let it be known that you are not alone. Be aware that we all have our own demons, some may be big, some may be small but they live inside us all and the best thing you can do for yourself is to acknowledge them. Shit, you should seriously even congratulate them for being so strong and tackling you down for the moment's notice. But don't you dare let it take ahold of you completely; you are not out of the fight.

Fight the good fight.

The hardest thing I have endured so far in my life wasn't suffering through my back injury or the surgery itself. It hasn't been any of my multi-day events or any race that I have done so far, not even dealing with my eating disorder or depression, nah, none of that was as hard as saying 'help me'.

Asking for help and admitting that I have a problem was without a doubt the hardest thing for me to do. To become that vulnerable to the world, to look at my family and expose something so dark, to admit to myself that I am struggling and I can't do this alone, was extremely hard. It was an outrageous throb that pushed me down onto the ground, spat all over my face, kicked dirt in my eyes.

This is you, this is you breaking down and this is you being a human. Slip into reality already, you are bulimic.

BITE YOUR LIP; SWALLOW.

I finally stopped trying to be so strong for so many others and opened myself up. Infect me, I beg of you, I'm raw, I want to heal. Putting my problems out there for everyone to see, for everyone to judge and for everyone to compare to was the best thing for me to do as exotic and rare as it was, it soothed me knowing that my vulnerability can help change someone's life.

Seven months after opening up to the 'world' about my eating disorder and I finally got the courage to go to a therapist who is captivated by the power between my pain and body. Something so incredibly magical brews between the two that has tragically created me and even inside my own little intelligent head, I know this but have yet to take my own advice and congratulate my demons on their brute strength so that I can move on in life.

Nice try but I'm not done with you yet, I'm not quitting, ever.

Regardless of how much I ached to let bulimia go, I found it extremely hard to actually let go of my behaviors but within time, I found that therapy brings me some comfort from being able to talk to someone who for the most part understands me (and doesn't know me).

I discover myself smiling at my struggles and truly coming to the revelation that the pain I feel is just another moment in my life, the good times come and go just like the bad.

I held onto my bulimia because it's ingrained inside my head to live like this, that this pain I control yet I'm out of control, bulimia is that grain of sand in my shoe and I really need to change my shoes already.

My therapist also helps me realize that I have never experienced peace with my body and that pain is all I've ever known, it is the definition of comfortable to me and as sad as that sounds, I fear losing it due to seeing what happens to me without it, because after all it's all I've ever known.

It's still very weird for me to be reaching my hands out for help, I'm twenty-one and I see a shrink because I am ruining my life with food.

You ever hear of the saying, you can lead a horse to water but you cannot make him drink? Although the horse may be thirsty, he will not always obey your commands even if it is obvious it will help him, he has to want to drink, he has to want to better himself. And as I was lead to the water, I looked across the glistening lily pads on its surface, the trees full of life and full of death surrounding me as I stood before my sip of destiny. Man, I sure do want to change, I want to be better, and I really do want to be healthy. So I dipped my head down and took a big gulp of water. It slid down my throat and even with the knowledge that it's good for me, my tongue tried to refuse it and I began to choke. The veins in my neck bulged, my legs stiffened up as my hands wrapped around my throat. Pure agony lasted a few seconds as I fought to accept it and before I knew it I forced the water down my throat.

Bite your lip; swallow.

Change is hard to come by willingly when it comes to a way of life you only know but I knew I needed to change it more than anything and besides, life can be painful sometimes, you know.

271

A full recovery is possible for anyone suffering from an eating disorder but it will never be completely away from you. For I am my own beacon and my own creation, my anorexia and bulimia helped sculpt me into the person I am today and I will never let that fade. I shine brightly due to my darkness and therefore I do not regret the pain as much as I hate it.

I have come to appreciate the teachings of my darkness and I encourage you to embrace your struggles with the approach and mindset of being a student. Like many students, you will find yourself failing a test from time to time, you will want to skip class or bad mouth your teacher, but be nice, you can learn from your demons, your teachers. If you take the time to find that courage to do so, then I guarantee you that one day you can manage them, you can call them out when they are present, and most importantly you can grow from them (and away from them).

It will always be a part of you in some way and you must learn how to manage that in your own unique approach and besides, you're worth it.

I highly suggest to anyone who struggles with an eating disorder or knows someone who does to seek the proper help and care that you or they deserve. But know that you will never technically 'be over' your eating disorder, cause you can never forget it. It is a part of you forever.

I also want to make a point of saying that becoming 'fit', 'shredded', 'cut', 'thin', 'lean', whatever you want to call it is not worth it if your health and sanity goes out the window. I beg of you to do your research on nutrition and training before you start any type of journey of weight-loss goals, doing a competition, or to just achieving overall better health. I beg of you to also make sure you're happy with whatever you do in life. I beg that, each day, you go to bed loving yourself and those around you because no one deserves to feel this pain.

Don't fall for the fads, the myths, the lies, and the bullshit, focus on number one, you. There is simply too much of that nonsense out in the world these days and it's making mental disorders become popular. It's something I'd like to see disappear and maybe with this book, I can help warn others like the few books that I picked up did.

Life for me has always been one misunderstanding thing to another and with each questionable ache I encountered, I bottled up more comfortably to having such pain in my everyday life. Oh how sick my mind had become, I had gone all this time labeling myself as a dark creature when in reality I was the brightest thing to enter a room.

My differences shined brightly with the patience to love myself, my flaws spoke in loud degrees of having acceptance, and my scars resembled more than just strength but the wisdom to never quit on oneself.

And do you know what the most astounding thing about all this is? We all can enter a room and our demeanor will speak this loudly too if we just believe in ourselves.

We must believe even when we do not believe because after all, it is a matter of how the light hits the trees....

I want to be something great.

I want to be something great.

I want to be something great.

One of the saddest things about my story to me was that I was already something great but I just didn't believe it, I didn't see it until I was left with nothing but my tears flooding my surroundings while the gut wrenching feeling of being ashamed and alone was the only thing I took notice of.

Greatness was already around me, I was already it, and it was always in my hands, I just needed to grasp it properly. I was so fixated on this impossible image that I had created inside my head of what greatness was that I couldn't even see it staring back at me in the mirror.

Now I can sit here and write about how I am actually a very happy person. I am one who is full of giggles and always seeming to be caught smiling even if a three hundred pound log is digging into my traps, I have only one shoe on, I haven't slept for days and I have only eaten jolly ranchers. I am also actually a very funny person.

In high school I was picked to be class clown out of my class, yeah, I'm just so silly. But after spilling the beans so to speak with this book, it appears that I am a very black and white person in terms of pain, that I am quite possibly one of the saddest individuals to get to know.

While all of this is very much the truth about me, that yes, I am a happy, funny, silly human who tolerates a lot of pain, at the same time I am a depressed, confused, and almost evil individual with my thoughts and I can't seem to handle my own head, but it is what makes me and I love it all.

All things Ella.

It wasn't easy to swallow at first but I've come to love it and instead of bashing on myself for my flaws, mistakes, and imperfections, I have accepted them, grown to appreciate them, and turned my never ending hauntings into a never ending drive to live a beautiful life.

But really, let's be real here, I'm also cool as shit man, just hug me.

Because you're worth it.

So, fight the good fight.

Bite your lip; swallow.

Become a beacon for yourself.

I couldn't care less what others have and will say of me. Although in the beginning of my career I ran myself face first into the ground, I got lost in the chaos, but with all my time spent in the dark, I have found my way through the darkness to fight on, to create more light for myself and for others.

I did not do this for the naysayers; I did not do this for pity, envy, or any other self-serving, biased bullshit. I did this so that I could possibly help save someone's life, move some souls, and educate those who are unaware of the extreme nature an eating disorder can be like. So that you can finally feel it, see it, know it and to be honest, I also wrote this because I simply love to write and express myself.

I've worked insanely hard to build myself, to create something great out of my strengths and weakness and as much as this self-induced labor seems to be geared towards my own personal release, I didn't think of just myself, I thought of the stories I have been told, the people I have met and haven't met, the support I received and the support I want to give.

During my times of denial about my issues, I wish I had someone to throw an inspirational book at me, help me find peace with eating again, get me the help that I needed so desperately; someone who was willing to just talk to me about my issues and actually know what it's like. I wish that I had a role model to look up to that admitted to such a struggle, who fought openly so that I could know that one day, I'll win my fight too.

Back then I felt like if I told someone about my eating disorder, I'd lose everything, I'd become viewed as weak, no one would like me anymore, and there would go my chances at reaching greatness. Ah, how all of that was such a gross, disgusting lie I told myself, like a little pig rolling around in mud, I was covered in this fear of the truth and it was just easier to cover myself up. Oink oink, I ended up shaking my thick layers of mud off my skin, even if it was dried, I decided to be done with it, look at me, I struggle with an eating disorder!

I want my limitless love of accepting myself and my flaws to spread into others. See the beauty inside your imperfections, I want that passion to swell into your heart and make it beat a little bit faster. I want the discovery of you inner courage to blossom inside you, know that you're strong enough to do what you need to do in life and then some. I want you to truly appreciate the shoes on your feet, the warmth of your bed and clothes, the healthy spine in your back, the healthy mind that you posse, and I want you to find the true origin of your life and discover your life's passion.

I want you to just be as much as I want to be.

My story is still being written. In regards to my competitions, my health, my life, and all that jazz, I'm happy to announce that I am still out doing crazy things. I have a sweet contentment with my life and just how it is unfolding, it is always a process and enjoying it is a choice I've made myself accept.

I am the Ella everyone knows me to be, smiling like a little fool, cracking sexual jokes, dreaming of unicorns, listening to metal, laughing way too much for my own good, and lifting rocks through the woods.

My journey to becoming something great was accomplished well before this was ever written and I look forward to writing another book about the next few chapters of my life as I continue to keep molding into myself. In the process, I may get a little lost at times, fall down but I will never quit on myself and no medal, title, or check can replace the feeling of overcoming adversity.

I'm Ella Anne Kociuba and I will always fight the good fight.

Give me mud. Give me scars.

What does this mean and why have I repeated it so much?

What is this mud I speak of?

Mud is wet dirt, it's hardship, it's a lesson.

Mud is all the things I have battled against and all the things that I have fought for and will fight for.

What are these scars I speak of?

Scars are damaged tissue, they are stories, they are trophies.

Scars are all the things that I have won and all the things that I have lost.

Enjoy my story.

ABOUT THE AUTHOR

Ella Anne Kociuba was born on June 21, 1993 in Austin, Texas, USA.

From the age of 6, Ella grew up riding horses. She has competed in many endurance races on horses, 25 mile horse races and 50 mile horse races.

At the age of 13, she had major spinal surgery. She became anorexic by the age of 18 and bulimic by the age of 19.

She is known for being the youngest female ever to win a Spartan Race at the age of 18.

Since then, she has competed in: Spartan Races, Tough Mudders, GORUCK's, Death Races, SISU IRON, half marathons, Warrior Dash, Superhero Scramble, 5k's and some other obstacle races and road races.

Also she was the youngest female to be a part of the Spartan Pro Team for Reebok Spartan Race.

On July 31st, 2014, she graduated in Massage Therapy at Lauterstein-Conway Massage School

In November of 2014, she finished her first book, All Things Ella, and it will definitely not be her last.

http://www.ellakociuba.com/